YUP,

GOOD TIMES

A Stroll Down Memory Lane,

With "Rugged Knee" and Me

STAN CALLANTINE

Yup, Good Times © 2021 by Stanley Callantine

Published in the United States by:

OLD STONE PUBLISHING

Old Stone Publishing
Boise, ID 83714
info@oldstonepublishing.com

First Edition
ISBN: 9798494610546

Printed in the United States of America

Most characters in this publication are, or have been, living at one time. However, any resemblance to those persons, living or dead, is based on the memories of a person who sees life from a hilarious perspective and may not jive with the memories of said persons.

Preface

I started writing the Memory Lane stories several years ago for my friends on Facebook. One of those friends, Colleen Parris Nelson, compiled the stories, had them bound, and presented them to me. She encouraged me to continue writing stories and to have them published. Thank you, Colleen!! That was the beginning.

Many of the stories include the adventures I had with my younger brother, Rodney Dale Callantine AKA "Rugged Knee". We spent our time using our imaginations and exploring the woods and rivers near our home about a mile west of Three Forks, Montana. Some of the things we did weren't the smartest or safest things to do, but somehow, we survived and had a memorable time. I lost my brother in 2013. Due to some tragedies in his life, he didn't spend much time with his sons Rob and Tony when they were growing up. This book should give them a little more insight into their dad. My hope is that children who read the book might experience the joy to be found from playing out of doors without cell phones and computers. - Stanley

Foreword

As I sit up on a cliff overlooking the breaking waves of the west coast of Bali, Indonesia, I'm reflecting my father's book here in front of me. I fully realize I clearly inherited my zest for life from this man. You see, our lives feel a bit parallel in this moment for me. I love the wildness of Bali. The nature, mountains, waters, and the animal life that surrounds me. I breathe fresh air, hear wild natural sounds and see green earth about me... it's the simple life. The life in which today's food is figured out today, and the days consist of whatever adventures we will find ourselves in today, and tomorrow's problems...well, they are simply tomorrow's problems.

My dad's book is a beautiful breath of fresh air and a reminder that life really should be lived a bit simpler. The present is exactly that...a gift for us to appreciate right now and in this moment. In childlike faith and optimism, life is meant to be appreciated all the way down to the littlest miracle seen in a frog, the challenge a child has with a loose tooth, or coming home wet after a boy's day of adventures. And days are quite certainly meant to be spent sharing these adventurous stories of a curious boy who grew up in the simple 50's, during the "good ol' days" in Montana, with the silliest and the most humorous stories which will be told for years to come. And that is exactly the gift my dad has put together for you, here in this book, a collection of his childhood giggles. My brother, mother, and I... along with many many family members have laughed over these stories for decades. I believe this book to be something that can sit on any coffee table throughout the world and give joy to any human who picks it up. And I can tell you, my father's greatest joy was to put a smile on the face of any person he crossed paths with. It is my absolute honor to have completed this book for my father, and my only living regret is that he wasn't able to hold his book in his earthly hands. But you get to...and that would have been his greatest wish.

Please enjoy!
Nique Callantine

Good Times

Oct. 15, 2013

JUST A THOUGHT: Ya know, over the years I had considered a lot of things to be "no big deal". When I was in grade school playing in a basketball game and the time was running out, I made a basket from the other team's free throw line into our basket. Everyone thought it was great. AAAHHH!!!! I just figured...it was no big deal. Or when I came home from overseas and my 18-year-old wife and baby boy came running out on the air strip with other wives and families, AAAHHH!!!! It was no big deal. When my son or daughter would have a boo boo, AAAHHH!!! It was no big deal. Well, now that I am older, and a little wiser, I look back and realize... it really was a big deal. So many little, tiny things in life actually really ARE a big deal for someone. If you have a small chance, then make life a little better for someone else by making things a little more of a big deal. It could bring joy to someone for a moment. It really doesn't take much.

Part 1: Growing up in Montana

***

My little cousin Gary used to be pretty cool. He was a lot younger than I was, but he had three other brothers, so we just picked the one closest to our age and that was the one that we hung out with when we visited, or they visited. We would all get together and play cowboys and Indians or somethin. But this littler guy had us over a barrel all the time. He always wore an old towel around his neck that hung down the back like a cape. He was in his own little superhero world, but the problem was, he really felt he was invincible.

"Taaa Daaa, I can never get hurt." I remember one day we set him up, he was always the last one when we were running, and the plan was to run him past the corner of the house and have a pillow there so we could whop him with it when he came by. I was always the leader because I could run faster than they could. So, we sat a pillow around the corner when Gary wasn't lookin, and we were messin around the garage and then the time came to do him in. You could always tell when Gary was comin because he always hollered, "UNDER DOG" and would run so his cape would fly behind him. Gary's problem was he ran so slow his cape just kinda hung there and his arms going back and forth was what made the cape move a little. Every other step was, "UNDER DOG, UNDER DOG, UNDER DOG". We all headed around the house and we could hear, "UNDER DOG" as Gary is bringing up the tail of all the kids. Everyone has already come around the house and is standing behind me up against the house, Ohhhh!!! this is going to be cool. Now I have the pillow and we can hear Gary comin, "UNDER DOG, UND"... CAWHOP! That kinda laid poor Gary out flat on his back, he didn't even finish his "...ER DOG". He lay there for a minute, nothing but his little eyes buggin out, then, we all started laughin so hard, Gary joined in and wasn't hurt at all. After all, you can't hurt "UNDER DOG".

Yup!!! Good Times.

***

I would like to dedicate this story to Elois Myers Johnson, Kathleen and Ed Jorgenson, and Linda Meyer Ehlers.

When I was a little kid, our family struggled at times to have enough money to buy food. But we lived in a beautiful little town where people cared about others and would help out. This little town was Three Forks, Montana.

I think when I was five or so, it had a population of around 1000 people. Great people. They maybe didn't know it, but to us they were great. Sometimes we wouldn't have much to eat, but if people from town knew that, they would help us out. Anyway I remember one of my favorite people was our barber Mr. Boots Meyers. He always treated me just like a grown up, even though I was only five or six. One summer I needed to get a haircut and mom put it off for as long as she could because she didn't have the 25 cents it cost. She evidently found a quarter somewhere. I found myself in the bathtub takin' a bath, with mom standin' over me makin' sure my hair was clean so it wouldn't dull Mr. Boot's clippers. I don't remember why, but mom seemed to be in a hurry. She washed my hair and rinsed it, but I was pretty sure all the soap wasn't out because I could still hear bubbles on the last rinse. But you know how moms are.

"There is still soap in my hair, mom."

"No, it's all rinsed out. Hurry up, I need to get to town."

I know one thing... not to sit and argue with mom, especially when you're naked and in the bathtub where you can't run anywhere. So, yup, she's right. It's all out.

So, we get to town and she drops me off at Mr. Boot's Barber Shop. There I am, 6-years-old I reckon. I remember looking at the strap hangin' off the back of his barber chair that he strapped his razor on to keep it sharp when the big guys were in there. It's a sound you don't forget, because you think he's going to shave you with that razor.

When Mr. Boots finished his last customer, he picked up a board that is padded on one side and laid it across the barber chair arms. He sat me on it and threw a sheet around me, pinning it behind my neck. "How would you like your hair, Stanley?" he asked.

"Uh, ah, uh." I was tryin' to say something.

Mr. boots saw me struggling a little and says, "I think I know." He wet my hair down and yup!! There ya have it, I can hear those bubbles that mom said we left at home. I heard Mr. Boots giggle a little and he spun the barber chair around to show me. In the mirror I saw white fluffed-up stuff all over my head.

He said, "Was your mom in a hurry today?" Before I could say anything, he said, "Oh, that's right, she did say she was in a hurry."

Mr. Boots finished washin' my hair and gave me my hair cut. I stayed in his barber shop and he talked to me just like I was a big guy until my mom came to get me. I saw my mom try to pay Mr. Boots, but I'm pretty sure he didn't take my mom's money. I think Mr. Boots knew we didn't have much.

He is a great guy. I love Mr. Boots, and the cool thing is...that was over 57 years ago. I bet, if you ask Mr. Boots, he probably remembers it today. Mr. Boots is still there. Not cutting hair though.

Yup!!! Good Times.

***

My little brother never, ever thought of the outcome of something before trying it.

He was about 8 years old, I reckon, and we had just come home from town where he and I had been sellin' some pop bottles at Hamilton's grocery store.

We had saved up a couple dollars over the past couple weeks and was wonderin' what we were gonna buy. Two bucks went a long ways back then. It was close to July 4th, so we had a lot of options. Firecrackers were pretty cheap and fun. We always unraveled our firecrackers, so it was easy to get to the next one. I always put mine in my pocket. Rugged-Knee, on the other hand, put his in a soup can. We were sittin' in an old 46 Plymouth coupe that was parked out back of the house a ways, lightin' fire crackers and tossin' them out the winda, tryin' to hit a coffee can about ten feet away. Whilst tossin' firecrackers out the winda in a 46 coupe, it is wise to roll the winda all the way down. Rugged-Knee did not. He had lit a few and tossed them, coming in close proximity to what he was trying to blow up out there. So because he was close, now he thinks he is the king of firecracker tossin'. But, the 10th one hit the edge of the winda and bounced back in his lap. I bailed out the driver's side fast and watched the scene unfold.

Unfortunately for Rugged-Knee, those Old 46 Plymouth doors were worn out and didn't unlatch like they used to. He jerked on the handle of the door a few times and decided his best option was to move. Rugged-Knee was all over the inside of that car trying to get away from that firecracker and he kinda spread a few more around. There was a lot goin' on and Rugged-Knee was cleanin' every winda in the car tryin' to get away from the action. The paper from them exploding firecrackers looked like he had hit the lottery with confetti flyin' all over. I'm not sure how many went off, but when Rugged-Knee finally got out of the window cleanin' business, he only had half a soup can of firecrackers left. Smoke was pourin' out of the half-down windas and there was a distinct odor of gun powder. I reckon he finally spied the door I had left open for him from the beginnin'. He had confetti stuck in his ears and his shorts at the same time. His glasses were cocked sideways, down to the tip of his nose.

Dad always said he thought there might be somethin wrong with him. He sure was fun to mess around with...just gotta keep him away from firecrackers. Everyone needs a Rugged-Knee.

Yup!!! Good Times.

***

When I was in the 8th grade, my mom thought if I went to school in Willow Creek, I might learn somethin'. She didn't know how wrong she was. It seemed to be the only thing I cared about was playing basketball with a ball that would hold air for more than 30 minutes. So, she sent me to Willow Creek because my older brother Ed went to school there and conveniently, he could drive us all to school. It was about 6 or 7 miles to school and my brother always thought he had to drive 100 MPH. It was a scary 15-minute ride. One day his 55 Chevy wouldn't start so we had to take mom's 1962 Pontiac station wagon. This is a pretty cool car. It was light purple with a white top and about 3 miles long. My older brother thought it was the fastest thing in Gallatin Valley. Once you got that sucker rolling, it seemed to smooth the road right out. Ed thought it had high performance hub caps or somethin. It had a plastic piece in the center of the steering wheel that the horn ring was attached to. It was concave and looked kinda like a coffee cup with a horn handle. OK, it wasn't quite that big, but good sized. So, when we headed off to school that morning, Ed was drivin' like normal, flooring it every time you take off so gravel flies all over. This only happens when we are out of sight of the house. As we get closer to the Willow Creek highway, we are going slower...I thought there was something wrong with the car. We finally made it to the highway and had started going about 60 when stuff broke loose on the driver's side...behind the steering wheel. Cool! My older brother was sick and threw up all over. That stuff came out of his mouth about 87 MPH, filled the steering wheel cup on the horn ring, and clouded his field of view with plastered used oatmeal all over the windshield. Probably one of the coolest things I'd ever seen. Not one thing in the car to clean it up with. He's not feelin' very good I reckon, but if he doesn't hurry up, we are going to be late. He managed to get us to school and headed back home.

Yup!!! Good Times.

***

Ya know I remember doing some pretty goofy stuff when I was young. One day in the winter, it was pretty cold out, but the sun was shining and it kinda had a warmth to it. Heck, I even had my coat unzipped. I was out looking for something to do by myself as my kick in the side, Rugged-Knee, didn't want to leave the house. So, I was on the prowl all by myself. I headed over to the gravel pits about a half mile from the house to see how the ice was. I got over there, and the ice was really smooth and clear, except that big open hole in the middle of the pond. I could see all the way to the bottom...about 8 ft deep. It was pretty thin out by the edge where that hole was, so I didn't get too close. It looked inviting though, so I decided to satisfy myself and go swimmin'. Summer was way too far to wait for a good swim. Even in the summer when you ask your mom, and she says no and you go anyway...she catches ya. Now, she will not even think I went swimmin' when it's cold out like this. So, I stripped down to my BVDs after I had broken the ice so I could climb back out. Geez, that water is cold! Now that I'm in... I'm ready to get out but I have to do one thing first...swim under the ice. Yup, this is going to be quick, and I can say I did it! I'm already frozen, so it isn't going to matter now. I take a deep breath...swim under the ice a little, look up to see what it looks like, and swim back to the open hole to get out. That was just so stinkin' neat! Now I am numb and really cold. I take off my BVDs, ring them out, stick them in my pocket, get dressed and head for the house. My mom will never know I went swimming without her permission. Fat chance. When I stepped into the house, mom noticed that my hair was frozen solid. Some things you forget about I reckon. I had a lot of answers to give to questions like "why is your hair frozen and why are your shorts in your coat pocket?". But hey, what do you do? You tell her the truth...you just couldn't resist that little dip in the pit and you found out that the ice looks the same on both sides.

***

My little brother, AKA Rugged-Knee, was not very athletic when we were young. Heck he wasn't very athletic when we were old either. The only thing he could do well was run real fast when he was scared. I kinda taught him how to do that.

I remember playing football with him. It was just him and me. We would pretend to hike the ball because there was no one else to receive it and then try to get to our makeshift goals. We didn't have money for a ball, so I spent a little time making one out of some old shirts and a pair of britches. Kinda cool. I cut off part of a pant leg and filled it with rags and tied each end with baling twine. I tied twine from one end to the other so the tie wouldn't slip off. When I needed more "air" in it, I added another old shirt. I was pretty fast in those days, but I guess I wasn't fast enough to catch a pig to make a real football. This one worked well though.

Rugged-Knee was a kick in the pants to tackle so I would foul up a tackle quite often so he would keep playing with me. I was so stinkin' fast, I could pass the ball and be there to catch the pass...so I really had the advantage on him. Oh yeah, and about a foot taller helped. He would get so mad he would yell at me. Most of the time, when he was tired of playing, he would say, "I have to go to the bathroom." I would say, "OK, I'll just practice kicking the ball while you're gone." Well, after about 30 minutes of kickin' the ball around, I decided to see where he was. Heck, I'm ready to rumble again. He never even went to the bathroom; he just went in the house and was goofing off. He left me out there playing football all by myself. That little weasel fibbed to me. I said, "Soo, aren't you going to come out and play some more?"

"NO, I don't have anyone on my team to catch the ball."

"So, I guess the game is over?"

He said, "Yes."

I said, "Well, OK, I win Ya know. I was going to let you win this one, but since you quit, you lose."

The sad thing is, I fell for this, 'I have to go to the bathroom' story more than once.

Yup!!! Good Times.

***

I remember my little dog Herman, an Australian Shepherd. He was pretty stinkin' cool. When his rear end itched, he would drag his rear end across the lawn. He didn't care who was around, it was just what Herman did. Mom would yell at him all the time "HERMAN, QUIT THAT!" Kinda funny.

My little brother Rugged-Knee, was pretty stinkin' cool as well. He didn't drag his rear end across the grass like Herman, but mom gave him the same treatment, "RODNEY QUIT THAT."

We really didn't have a lawn at our place, Herman thought we did though. It was just the hay that was close to our house was cut with a lawn mower instead of a tractor, seemed to trick him. That was one of my jobs to do in those times I could actually get the lawn mower to start.

This was on my "to-do" list one day. I really had other things to do, and I wasn't really into mowing. I tried to get the mower to start, and it wouldn't, so I checked the gas and the oil and pulled the starting cord about 20 dang times. It was one of those ropes that had a knot in the end. You had to wind it around a pulley and pull, then do it again if it didn't start. I think my dad got it at the city dump, not sure. So, I went into mechanic mode. I wasn't sure it was getting any spark, the thing should have run. I was pretty smart back then, and knew all about mowers...except this one.

My little brother Rugged-Knee was right there to help me out. I talked him into grabbing hold of that spark plug while I pulled on the rope to see if it had any juice to it. I'd have held onto the spark plug, but he couldn't pull the cord fast enough and I couldn't do both at the same time.

"Hey, Rugged-Knee, grab that spark plug for a second."

Rugged-Knee is smarter than I thought, "I ain't goin ta grab that spark plug," he said.

"OK I'll pull the spark plug wire and you grab just the wire."

"Nope, it's going to shock me."

"OK, here." I handed him Herman, "You just hold Herman's foot on there, while I pull on this cord."

"OK!!!"

I pulled on the rope as hard as I could, and the engine whizzed around like nobody's business.

"YUP!!! WE HAVE SPARK."

Herman was howling and running like a cat getting baptized, headed out behind the shed about 75 ft away. Rugged-Knee was howling and pickin' himself up a few feet away and had a bunch of choice words for me whilst headin' into the house. I'm laughing so hard my eyes are leakin' and I know mom will be out in a second. Herman took my hiding spot, so I need to be ready. Yup!!! Here she comes.

"STANLEY WHAT THE HECK DID YOU DO?" Mom used another word instead of HECK, but it did start with an 'H'.

"I was just trying to start the lawn mower and Rod was helping and he must have gotten shocked or somethin."

I have to say that Rugged-Knee got me in more trouble.

Yup!!! Good Times.

***

When Halloween came around, I can remember only Rugged-Knee and I trick or treating. My older siblings must have been too stinkin' old or somethin'. My mom would drop Rugged-Knee and I off in town with our 'get ups' on to get some candy. We didn't have any money back then for uptown fancy costumes, but we did the best we could with what we had.

Rugged-Knee always had a ghost outfit with two holes in an old sheet, every stinkin' year he did that. I finally told him that I wasn't going to go with him if he was still going to wear that same old sheet. He was 27 when I put my foot down. Me, I always went with the bum look, yup!!! (I still look like that, but don't get any candy for it.) I wore my regular clothes, with the hole in the knee and dad's old shirt and hat. Mom used to put coffee grounds on my face for whiskers. She would put lard on my face with a trowel, then slap used coffee grounds on there. My friend David Phillips got fresh coffee grounds. I love the smell of fresh coffee, so we followed David around everywhere he went, sniffin his coffee.

We had our sacks about half full of candy by the time we headed for home. While we walked down the back road, I figured out that if I scared the heck out of Rugged-Knee and got him screamin' and runnin', he would spill half his candy on the road. Someone could just walk up the road later and pick it up, like you were at a parade and no one was there but you. So, I tried this out and oh my gosh!

I got home, grabbed a flashlight and headed back up the road where all the screamin' started. You would think I was at the candy store!

I had to hide it in the shed so Rugged-Knee didn't see it and put a claim on it.

Yup!!! Good Times.

Present day memory in the making

Holy Smoke, I knew it was coming to this, it was just a matter of time. With the government "shut down", from now on in Idaho, Montana, and Wyoming all the cattle guards have been laid off.

***

We used to have a lot of fun driving our old '36 Chevy PU around in the field. My older brother thought he owned it, but I knew better. I was pretty sure my dad owned it. I think whoever put the 2 gallons of gas in it at the time was the owner until they ran out of gas. On the fender, there was an indentation where the spare tire went and a bracket that held the tire in place. There was no spare tire to go there, so Rugged-Knee thought it was a great place to ride, squattin in that hole and hangin' onto the bracket. One day, dad needed some gravel, so my older brother, Ed, and I grabbed a couple shovels and headed for the bottom half of our field to get some. Ed is driving and as we go past the corner of the house, that little weasel Rugged-Knee came running at full speed around the corner of the house and jumped onto his favorite fender. This old truck isn't the smoothest thing to ride in, and we are bouncin around in the cab and the weasel is really hangin on. I told Ed to be careful, that Rugged-Knee was on the fender. Ed said, "I'll shake him off."

I told him he might run over him if he did that. Ed didn't seem to mind, he just wanted Rugged-Knee off that fender for some reason. So, he starts swerving back and forth, hitting badger holes and gopher holes tryin' to shake the weasel off. I'm lookin out the winda trying to see what Rugged-Knee was going through. I think he had Velcro on his tennis shoes, and super glue on his fingers. Finally, the little weasel had enough and decides to depart. He jumps straight up in the air, and I swear, I was lookin up at the bottom of his tennis shoes as he passed across the hood of the truck and across the windshield. I can't remember if they read "PF Flyers", or "Polly Parrot", but just as Rugged-Knee jumped, Ed made a hard-right turn and Rugged-Knee was cleanin' the windshield with his dirty old tee shirt. I saw him roll across the ground on the driver's side and Ed just kept pourin' the coals to the old Chevy. I'm bouncin' up and down on the passenger's seat tryin to see out the back winda, and what happened to Rugged-Knee. The last time I saw him he was runnin for the house. I don't know if he was tryin' to get to the house before mom saw what was happenin' or going to tattle on us. When we had the gravel we needed, I think Ed was a little scared to take it back to dad. I was just a passenger, I had nothing to do with this one, except yellin' out the passenger window tryin' to convince Rugged-Knee that it was probably in his best interest to jump. I bet mom and dad really hoped we would grow up and be responsible soon.

Yup!!! Good Times.

* * *

My friend Ralphie was a pretty cool kid. He came to my house every day and stayed all day. We used to do some pretty cool stuff together. Ralphie had his own car and smoked cigarettes and was only 13, I think. If Ralphie didn't come to my house, I would worry that somethin' was wrong. One time he came up missing for two days. When I asked him where he was, he said he drove over to Butte two nights before and stayed all night and day with his friend Eddie Tragija. Ralphie was a grown up kid.

One day, we were sitting in Ralphie's car talking and he started to smoke a cigarette and asked me if I wanted one. "Sure, I'll have one." So, we lit up and I took a few puffs and just as I was going to take another puff, the thing exploded!

Sparks and ta-backy flew up my nose and all over the place. I think it even parted my hair. As I'm slappin the sparks on my arm and face, Ralphie is over there just crackin' up. I still had that stub of a cigarette hangin' out of my mouth and dancing in the seat. I said, "Where did you get those cigarette loads?"

He said, "Couldn't find any cigarette loads, so these are cigar loads."

"Well, they sure blew the pajamas out of my cigarette" (idea brewing)… "hey, let's find Rugged-Knee."

Now, Rugged-Knee started smokin when he was about 6, I think. This is goin' to be pretty swafty. I kept Rugged-Knee busy while Ralphie plants one of those loads in the pack we knew he had hidden in the shed. So, it's a done deal and now everywhere Rugged-Knee went, Ralphie and I aren't too far behind. We're goin to see somethin pretty cool pretty quick. He heads out behind the shed so Ralphie and I sneak over behind the tractor to watch this ordeal unfold. Rugged-Knee lit it, and it exploded right away, I guess Ralphie didn't get the load in very far. So he is doin' a little jig and tryin' to yell, lookin around for Ralphie and I without losing his cigarette butt. There is a little stub stickin' out of his mouth and the match he had used is nowhere to be found. There is a black streak runnin up the side of his nose and he is cussin' up a storm. We finally give in and come out laughing' so hard we can't stand up. When Rugged-Knee calms down, he thinks it's pretty cool and wants to go stick one in mom's cigarettes. Hummm!!! Now that might be…

"Nope, I don't believe I want any part of this one." I would have liked to see it though.

Yup!!! Good Times.

***

I remember one day around 1963 or 1964, my dad came home from working with the horse races in Idaho, or Washington, or somewhere. I guess at the time it wasn't important to me where dad was, but by golly, he brought me a boomerang when he came home. Now this piece of wood is so dang cool once you figure out how it works. Dad slept in and that piece of wood was on the kitchen table when I got up. I remember looking it all over really closely. I ate my breakfast fast, snagged it and headed out in the field. I threw that thing so many times I felt like I had blisters on my fingers. That thing never came close to coming back. I took it back home after throwing it 20 acres and back, I reckon that's 40 acres total. I was ready for dad to get up so I could tell him he got ripped off. Dad finally made it up and showed me how it worked. Didn't know you had to throw it with the pointy end facing out. You also have to throw it down instead of up. Every time I threw it up, it would land 43 feet behind me. I threw that silly thing and it landed behind me every time. I finally got the hang of it though and decided to go gopher huntin' with it. Those ground squirrels would stand up lookin around out there in the field. I'd throw that boomerang and as it swished by them, they'd duck and run and that boomerang would come after me. I'd be watchin' what the gophers were doin' and forget about that dang boomerang. Well, after a couple days of this and me gettin' the heck beat out of me, I decided to throw it away. One last throw and I ran into the house. As far as I knew that thing was still out there flying around. A couple days later I grabbed my gun to get the gophers with. As I headed out, that dam boomerang landed not too far from me. Yup, Rugged-Knee had found it and came running around the corner of the house lookin' for it. I showed him how you are supposed to throw it and he threw it about two times and hit himself both times. Then he went squealing into the house. I guess I could take more of a beating then he could.

Yup!!! Good Times.

* * *

One year for Christmas, I received one of those little airplanes that has a motor and strings coming out of the wings so you could fly it in circles. I wanted to fly that thing so stinkin' bad, but there was a foot of snow out and nowhere to take off from. The plane was a P-40 with a three-blade prop and was supposed to fly really fast.

I sat in my bedroom and started it. In order to shut it off, it had to run out of gas. It had a little tiny gas tank, but it would run long enough that my mom came and yelled at me. Sometimes I would drop a dirty sock on the prop to shut it off.

One Saturday the sun was shinin'. My dad's friend, Harry came to our house. He had flown them before, so we went down to the picnic pond that was frozen over and smooth as glass.

This is going to be so cool. I'm wound up pretty tight, excited to try flying it after Harry got it started and warmed up. We fired it up and I scrambled out of the way. Harry had the controls and dad held the plane and let it go. Boy that sucker was fast. It made a half circle, went straight up into the air, then came straight down and nosedived at about 637 MPH into the ice! The engine shot 40 feet over to the edge of the ice and pieces and parts flew everywhere.

I think my heart was broken in just as many pieces. We gathered the airplane parts all up and put them in the box. Dad said he could fix it. Are you serious?? That P-40 that looked like Rugged-Knee had stuffed it through a meat grinder (we didn't have blenders back then).

Dad took the three-blade prop, now a one blade prop, and put a brand new 2 blade on it. A couple days later, dad had it all together ... the engine ran and everything.

I tried flying it once more, without Harry's help this time, but the two-blade just didn't give it enough power to get it off the ground.

I didn't see Harry again until spring. He must have felt bad.

It's OK Harry.

Yup!!! Good Times.

***

One spring day, after the tadpoles started turning into little frogs, I was lookin' for something to do so I went across our lane to Mr. Sprinkle's willows. There was always a bunny over there and water around the willows from the spring runoff. I was nosin' around and there weren't many frogs, but I did notice there were caterpillars everywhere. Hey, now these were pretty stinkin' cool! Both ends looked the same so you had to wait until they moved to see which way was forward. I don't think they had reverse, but they could turn on a dime and give you nine cents change. Kinda looked like an oreo cookie with a pumpkin middle. They had long hair all over them.

I wanted to show these cool things to Rugged-Knee. I caught two or three and put them in my pocket but by the time I got another one, there were only two in there. So, I kept catching them and after about 15 minutes, I finally had 6 in there. I held my pocket shut, runnin' for the house, over two fences and I got home with three! Those dang little things were jumpin' out on the way home! I headed for the bedroom to show Rugged-Knee and mom stopped me at the bedroom door. "How many of those caterpillars do you have?" Now it was really, really hard to sneak something past my mom.

"How do you know I have caterpillars?"

"Well silly, they are all over you. You go outside. I'll send Rodney out."

I must have had 50 of those little critters all over me. I thought it was funny. I had never seen a caterpillar jump. After we finished playing with them, we itched like crazy for a couple days.

I learned a lot from trial and error in those days. If things didn't bite, scratch, kick, or stink, they made you itch. The plants were just as bad as the animals.

Yup!!! Good Times.

***

When I was about 8 years old or so, my mom trusted me enough to let me sit by the back door in the car with the window rolled down. She even let me do this when the car was in motion! I thought it was cool to stick my arm out the window while going about 60 or so. If I held my hand horizontal and pointed my fingers up and the wind got under them, it would make my arm go up. Now how stinkin' cool is this? If I pointed them down, my arm would go down and in and out. Holy Cow... this is cool!! My dad said that you had to pull your arm in when a diesel truck came by or it would spit on your arm. Silly diesel. So, I have this arm flying thing under control. I'm havin' a lot of fun doing this until we get to our lane. We are going so slow now that there isn't enough air to make my arm go up and down and stuff, but there are a lot of really tall, pretty wild sunflowers growing along the lane. I think I'll just reach out and touch one. Oh Ya, that was cool. So cool, I'll pick one as we drive by. And mom is kina going a little faster at this point. Now, I have always liked challenges and going this speed, if I can just pop the head off of one of those sun flowers by grabbing it, it would make my day! So, I grabbed one. I don't think anyone on the face of the earth knew that wild sunflower heads are welded to the stem. This thing was like grabbin' a 1/2 in. steel rod with a car rim welded to it. It dang near jerked me right out of the car. Most of the cars back then didn't have seat belts and if they did, we never wore them. Now this came about so stinkin' fast I'm really not sure what happened. In a split second, my arm was pulled off and my face was slammed into the back of the front seat and then up against the door post between the front and back doors. I grabbed the window handle to keep from flyin out the winda. When I came to my senses, I wound up with three of those stinkin' yellow pedals between my fingers. I glanced over at mom and she didn't look at me or anything as she kept looking straight forward out the windshield. She did say, without looking or cracking a smile, "I bet that hurt." I'm pretty sure I saw her smile a little as we turned into the yard. I can't ever remember being beat up so fast in all my life. Heck, it always took my siblings a little longer to do this much damage to me. I bet mama was laughin' inside though.

Yup!!! Good Times.

***

 Well, when I was six or seven years old, my dad had his own logging outfit and we lived back up in the mountains of Montana. Dad would fell a lot of trees and then my older brother and I would limb them and roll them so dad could skid them down to the landing. Which means, he would put a cable or chain around one end of the logs and pull it down with a Cat tractor to a landing place that was big and wide enough to load them onto logging trucks. Well, I felt pretty stinkin' special and like a privileged character because my dad trusted me with a double-bladed axe. I could walk on those logs and cut the limbs off just as well as anyone, even big anyones. Sometimes I'd slip and fall off but that goes with the job. My dad said, "If you lose your balance or slip, get rid of the axe so you won't fall on it."

We had these log rollers that had a bent hook on one end. They kinda looked like a shovel with a big fishin' hook attached above the end. The hook would swivel up and down like a hinge and it had a sharp point like a fishin' hook. You lift the hook up over the log and as you push on the handle, the log rolls. If you do it right, you can work it like a ratchet and just keep going back and forth. It was pretty cool. But I remember one time the log rolled down hill, and with a little gravity helpin', that stupid hook on the log roller got caught in the log. The handle kina went up between my T-shirt and my suspenders. It happened so fast I couldn't react quick enough. My dad said that this is how accidents happen. Now I'm only six years old here and don't weigh much and I can see right now that I'm fixin' to get a beatin'. Yes sir, the log kinda had seniority over my little rear end at this point. Then the suspenders kinda acted like a catapult and launched me over the log and somehow, the elastic in the suspenders planted me on the other side of the log before the log roller made it. I swear that was like stepping on a rake three or four times real fast. There were enough pine boughs laying on the ground that it softened my landing. When the log rolled over me, it just pushed me down in the boughs face first and didn't hurt me too much, but felt kinda like going through a chipper shredder. I do remember sitting up afterwards and lookin' around to see if anyone saw. I was all scratched and beat up. The sad thing was, there wasn't anyone around to blame it on!

Yup!!! Good Times.

***

I used to have a lot of fun scarin' the heck out of my little brother Rugged-Knee. I don't know why it is so stinkin' funny to scare someone. They jump because they aren't expectin' it. For me, I just can't help myself and I bust out laughin'. Rugged-Knee was my prime target, because you could scare him, and he would just come unglued. He would run with no idea where he was goin' and after he got there, he didn't know why he was there. Give him five minutes and scare him again and he would go back where he came from. I've seen chickens do that. I have tried scarin' a lot of others, but it's just not the same.

I scared my mom a few times and she has no control over her reflexes. I used to get the same thing every time I scared her. She would jump and yell at the same time and then proceed to slap the heck out of me. I used to spend a lot of time runnin' from my mom. The good thing was mom was only good for about eight or nine steps before she gave up.

Now my sister, Lanette was a different story. She would jump like a surprised cat, come off the floor about twice her height, scream, and look for somethin' to throw while poundin' on me. I always thought I could get her to bang her head on the ceiling. The problem was, she would hold a grudge. Yup, eventually she was going to get even. She would come in when I wasn't expecting anything, like when I was brushin' my teeth or getting a drink of water and just flat slap me around, I thought, for no stinkin' reason. But she would always come up with a reason. "You had that comin."

"What? I didn't do anything."

"That was for last week."

"Awhhh jeez!!!!"

So, whenever I scared her, I decided to just stand there and take it. I'd let her get in a couple good licks and it would be over (Sometimes). I guess it was just how she felt at the time. If I didn't get a beatin' right then, I'd walk like I was sneakin' across a floor covered with corn flakes, peak around corners before steppin out. I don't think she liked me. I tell ya, I was really good with that sneakin' thing. I felt like I was in training to scare Rugged-Knee. Rugged-Knee put a lot of miles on his tennis shoes getting away from mountain lions, bobcats and hairy women. Cripes, even Herman peed all over because I scared him. So much for a watchdog huh?

Yup!!! Good Times.

***

A star is born: When I was little, my side kick Rugged-Knee and I used to just plod around lookin for stuff to get into. We did a pretty good job of it. The biggest problem was, ...Rugged-Knee was 4 1/2 years younger than I, so I was always the one that did it first. I remember one time when Mom and I went up to Bozeman. Mom parked out behind the hospital and left me in the car. Now this is OK because I haven't yet become the Stanley we know today. We had just moved from Pipestone, Montana to Three Forks, Montana so everything was new to me and I'm only 4 1/2 years old anyway. It seemed like Mom was in that big building for a long time. When she came out, she had something that looked like a pile of blankets. Well, by golly, there was a little tiny kid in there and he was makin' a bunch of racket screamin and stuff. I do remember askin' Mom if we could keep him though. Later, those words, "Look what I found, can we keep him?" would haunt and scare my mom for years and years. Now I'm startin' to get used to havin' this little critter around and can't wait for him to get bigger so I can take him outside. This kid is kinda cool, but sure is cranky. If he doesn't get his way, he throws a fit, screams, cries and is just plain obnoxious. I'm five now and I'm pretty sure when he is old enough to go outside, I can fix this little problem. So, I guess I just have to wait for a few years. Mom lets him come outside when he is not even two, but boy is he a plump little thing and can't even walk yet. I can start breakin him in though with this little bouncy chair he is in out on the lawn. If I sneak up behind him when he is squealin' and throwin' one of his little fits and pull real slow on the back of that springy chair until I think the chair is going to fall over, then turn it loose, I might launch his plump little butt out of that chair and that will give him somethin' to yell about...or he will quit yelling. Just as I was about to turn loose, mom showed up from behind me. I have no idea where she went, and I have no idea where she came from, but this is the first of my lessons in "slappin' the heck out of Stanley 101". Yup, I received quite a few more lessons over the years and I don't think I ever passed the course. My wife later took over where my mom left off, so I am still in training.

Yup!!! Good Times.

***

I remember my grandpa shaking a lot. I didn't understand it when I was little, but my mom told me he had Parkinson's disease. I reckon that is when you can't hold still. He always sat in a recliner-like chair. It never reclined back in those days, but it did rock back and forth. It squeaked some when he rocked in it. He would sit next to the dining room table and read. He shook so much I couldn't understand how he read when his book was movin' around like that. I thought grandma put his cup on a saucer so she could tell where he was because of the clatter when he was on vibrate like that. I thought my grandma was the smartest lady west of the Mississippi River to think of this way to keep tabs on grandpa. Mama kept telling me it was to catch the coffee grandpa spilled when his cup was full.

Grandma had one of those coo-coo clocks and one day at 12 noon, the bird came out coo-cooin'. Grandpa was rockin' with the squeakin' chair and tryin' ta set his cup on the saucer. It sounded pretty cool, it didn't seem like it was long after that that the hit song, Rockin' Robin came out. My mama had always loved music and could play a few different kinds of musical instruments, I'm pretty sure grandpa influenced her when she was younger. Who would have ever thought I had a rock-n-roll grandpa?

Yup!!! Good Times...

***

When I was 12 years old or thereabouts, Rugged-Knee and I was tryin' ta keep a balloon in the air in the living room without it touchin' the floor. Whoever missed the balloon and let it touch the floor, was poison. Yup, you didn't want to be poison or you would be poison until you died and that wasn't good. You would always have to eat alone. We got so good at it, we decided that the balloon couldn't touch the furniture either. Oh, yeah, we had to move in slow motion. Rugged-Knee was pretty good at waiting till the balloon almost touched the couch and he would save the day and get it in the nick of time.

He dove for the balloon once and the slow-motion thing shifted into high gear. The trickster dove to the couch and tried to do a somersault and hit the balloon so hard it flew between his legs and up to the ceiling. Ha! In the middle of his somersault, as his leg went up his shoe came off and he launched it clear across the room. It cleaned off everything that was on the bookshelf. I heard mama head that way from the kitchen and I headed for my bedroom. Mama was right up to his face when she asked Rugged-Knee what the heck was goin' on. Rugged-Knee was still a little dopey I reckon. It hadn't registered what had happened yet. I reckon he was still in slow motion mode and the only thing in fast motion was his shoe and his older brother. Mama felt it was her sworn duty to find out why he cleaned everything off her bookcase from across the room. I heard his reply as I was peeking through the tiny crack in the door. It was pretty hard to beat. "I didn't do it!"

Hey! Wasn't me! I wasn't even in the room that long. I know when to get out of Dodge and to put some real estate between me, Rugged-Knee, and the bookshelf. I had a lot of practice I reckon.

Rugged-Knee wound up restockin' the shelf, Mama went back to whatever it was she was doin and me, well.... looks like I am goin' to be poison until I die.

Yup!!! Good Times.

***

To write about this whole trip... I will have to tell two stories. First when I was fourteen years old, my dad, two of his friends, my older brother, one of his friends and I all went deer huntin' out by Maudlow, Montana in our "huntin' buggy", my dad's 1951 two door Caddy. Yup!!! Mom didn't want dad and his cronies and kids to wreck her car up in the mountains, so this Caddy was the only thing we could carry everyone in.

We left our house early in the morning, about 4:00 AM, stop to pick up Ed's friend in Three Forks and then stop in Manhattan to pick up dad's two friends and off into the mountains we go! Now this is a two deer area, so with all of us, we can get 12 deer total. The place we are going is also where dad is logging at the time. There is a locked gate we have to go through just off 16-Mile Canyon Road, but dad has the keys to it. We drive through the gate and up the road a little ways. Dad let us younger boys out while he and his pals went on up the road. Dad said to just keep going up this canyon till you come to our logging camp. I have no idea where Ed and his buddy went, but I went over the hill and up the canyon. I didn't see anything, and I walked about a mile. It's so stinkin' cold! About zero degrees, I reckon. Anyway, I have about 3 layers of clothes on... an orange vest on over my coat, 3 shirts, and dad's coveralls. I have a pair of old green pack boots along with three pairs of socks and an Elmer Fudd hunting hat with the ear muffs down over my ears. I'm packin' my dad's old 303 Savage, Model 99 rifle that had the stock broke off one time, so it had some black electrical tape to help hold it together. Now the barrel of this old gun is longer than I am... a 303 Savage bullet basically flies in slow motion. It travels at about 37 ft per second. Anyway, I have so much stuff on I can't hardly move and I'm looking across this clearing, planning my next move. The clearing is about 200 yards across to a line of trees that follows a creek bed on the other side. Then I hear something! I turn around and there is my dad standing right behind me. He said, "Sit right here on this stump for about 10 minutes. The other guys are coming this way and there will be a herd of about 50 deer run through this clearing." Hot damn! I'm ready. I sit there for what seemed like 6 hours, but it was only about 5 minutes. I stand up and throw my sling over my shoulder as I'm thinkin' "There aren't 50 deer comin'...there aren't even 50 deer on this whole mountain." So, I head out across the clearing through the 10 inches of snow. "I bet there aren't 15 deer on this stupid hill! Probably not even 5! In fact, I bet no one has even seen 5 deer yet!!!" (to be continued)

Yup!! More Good Times Comin'!!!

***

At this point, I'm kinda' in a trance. I am so angry that those stupid deer didn't receive the memo that they were supposed to run across this clearing that I'm standing in. I suddenly catch a movement to my left and I turn to see what it is...it might be those stupid deer. Yes! Yes! Yes! There they are! Right on time, it turns out. And they are right there in the open, about 30 feet away. By the time the shock leaves my system, they have realized they could be in trouble here. The lead doe makes a sharp left turn. Holy moly, I'm grabbin' for the gun I have slung over my right shoulder. With big old mittens and all those clothes, I'm strugglin' a little. My thumb goes under my vest when I grab my sling. Now my vest is coming with the gun and my coat slips so it's not on straight. I'm sayin' a few choice words at this point. The barrel of that old 303 hits the back of my head and knocks Elmer Fudd's hat cattywampus. When I look down to see how to get rid of the vest that seems to have a hold of my gun, the ear flap that was keepin' my ear warm is now over my eye! I jerk my gloves and my hat off so I can see. I finally get that old gun up with the safety off. Now, you have to take into consideration that this all happened in about 3 seconds and by now I'm standing out there in the clearing looking like I'm guarding a pile of clothes. It's a good thing that old gun finally released itself from my vest or I very well could have been standing out there in my shorts. When this whole thing started, there were at least 50 deer...maybe more! With all the excitement, fast-moving Stanley and clothes flying all over, the deer didn't seem to want to stick around to see if I was going to make it down to my shorts or not. They probably thought I was goin' for the big guns. So now I'm ready and there is only one deer in sight, a 4-point buck. He's trailing the herd about 100 yards away and still puttin' some real estate between him and that pile of clothes. I don't remember aiming at him, but I had the gun pointed in his general direction. He was makin' very good time and he jumped over a log just as I pulled the trigger. I didn't see where he went, I just watched to see if any of the deer would show up on the other side of the tree line. They didn't, so I gathered up my laundry and ran over to the creek bed and over the little knoll to see if any deer had hung around a little. Nope, just a creek bed full of deer tracks. I turned to walk back to the clearing, chewin' myself out for not staying as long as dad said, but heck, I didn't have a watch. I heard a gasping noise, looked around, and saw that buck! He evidently felt sorry for me and had jumped into my bullet, after all. Deer can do that ya' know, when your bullet is so slow. He may have just tripped over that log and knocked the wind out of himself while he was lookin' over his shoulder watchin' a goofy kid chasin' him with an arm load of clothes and an old gun. Yup!!! I think I would run too.

More Good Times Comin'!!!

***

 My mom found this little kid hangin' around the hospital in Bozeman, Montana when I was only around four and a half. I called him Rugged-Knee after he was a few years old because he spent the majority of his time on his knees and was pretty hard on britches. The kid was always yelling. Mom said it was because of me. One thing about Rugged-Knee, he was a built-in experimentation station. I could just about talk him into anything. The key words were, "come on, this is going to be super swafty," or "pretty nifty," or just flat "cool!" So anyway, one year it was pretty cold outside, and we only had single pane windows in the house. When it is cold outside and warm inside, the inside has moisture, so Jack Frost goes to work and paints all kinds of pictures on the windows. It's pretty stinkin' cool. The rule was, "Don't touch the window!". Rules weren't put out there to be ignored ya know. So, I obeyed all the rules my momma put out there for us kids. I guess there was a little sneakin' around, but for the most part, I was a good kid. It was that Rugged-Knee kid that gave her grief! He used to dink around the windows when they were all frosted up. He would put his hand on the top where the frost was the thinnest and kinda melt the frost with the heat of his hand. Now I remember that mom said NOT to touch the windows. It's kinda funny what little kids do when they know they aren't supposed to do somethin' and they think they are sneakin' around. The window has their complete attention. Then someone a little older, who knows better, catches them in the act. By this time in my life, I'm pretty sure this kid is related to me. So, the best thing to do is save him from my mom's wrath, just in case she enters the room. So, I kinda snuck up behind him so mom couldn't hear me save him. Yup, got right behind him and smashed that paper bag I had filled with air against my other hand. KA POW!!! It amazes me what the human body is capable of doing in midair, once it is launched from the couch. I think the air to lips ratio is pretty high as well from the amount of cuss words I didn't realize a six-year-old had. Yup!!!, Like a flash of lightning my mom came running in the room to see what was going on and I received a few more choice words. Kinda funny how one thing leads to another. Gosh, I was just keepin the window from breakin'.

Yup!!! Good Times.

***

 Back in the early 60's, us kids used to go out in the winter when it was real cold out and walk along the edge of the shed and the house and knock the icicles down. It would take about two weeks for them to grow big enough for us to reach them with our hands. If we couldn't reach them it was time to drag out a big stick. These foot-long icicles were good stuff to suck on. It used to be a race to see who could get the most icicles knocked down before someone got hit on the head with a chunk of ice. But one thing I found out. If it's pretty cold out and your hands are a little wet when you get a hold of one of those icicles, you have a hard time turnin' loose of that sumbitch. Now this is where I got the idea to introduce and educate Rugged-Knee to what I have found out. The best way to do this without trickin' him into it is to take his mittens away and give him a small icicle to suck on. Yup!!! And he has no idea what is going to happen when his hands melt the ice, and they get a little wet. I have saved another icicle for him too. Now this icicle is the best icicle this side of the Mississippi River. It is right over by the shed and it is about 3 feet long and just as perfect an icicle as the good Lord could ever give me. I took it off the house earlier and stashed it so my sister and older brother wouldn't trash it. So Rugged-Knee is suckin' on the little one and I said, "Come check this one out. If you can pick it up without your mittens, I'll give your mittens back to you and you can go show mom the icicle." How stinkin' cool is that? Holy Smokes! He picked it up and couldn't turn loose of it and the kid freaked out on me. Did you know sound travels a long way when you live in the country where it's pretty quiet and someone bellows out really loud? Rugged-Knee was not calm about this whole situation. Talk about getting excited! He bellowed like grandma's milk cow and jumped up and down. Cripes, you would have thought I slammed his hand in a door or somethin'! It always amazed me that my mom was surprisingly quick like a panther, even being overweight. It was 100 feet out to the shed, but she was all over me like a cat on a hot tin roof. In my defense, I had plans to help him out of his situation with some hot water but didn't expect him to come unglued like that. A couple things I learned about mom. I don't think I was her favorite child, I thought I could outrun her, and thought she might calm down a little by the time she got to me. That didn't happen too often. But I have heard her giggling sometimes on stuff I did.

Yup!!! Good Times.

***

Sometimes it's really hard when you are little and your feelings show.

One year I bought a little yellow chick at Easter time. Well, I really didn't buy it. I bought a little bag of chicken seed for 49 cents and they threw in the chicken for nothin'. I gave Rugged-Knee some money and he bought another bag of seed and received a twin to my chicken. So anyways, we took them home and turned them loose in the yard.

My dad built a garage out by the side of our house one year. He never put a car in it for very long though, just when he worked on one. I would say it was more of a shop than a garage. It had a bench at the far end of it that had dad's tools and stuff on it. Dad used to be gone on the weekends at the racetrack and home sometimes during the week. I used to get an ass chewin' sometimes because when God invented chickens, he installed a secret code of some sort that said they had to roost in order to sleep. For some reason, these (now) chickens, took over dad's garage and claimed it for their club house, AKA Chicken Coop. There was no overhead door on the garage, so it was free homesteadin' for the chickens. They liked to roost there, up and out of the way from the monsters and bigfoot that roamed around.

Now I didn't see a problem with it, thought it was pretty cool. Dad, on the other hand, didn't like that brown and white stuff all over his bench and tools. Dad said that stuff was "chicken shit". He said that white stuff mixed in with the brown was "chicken shit" too. He didn't care what color it was; he didn't like it all over his stuff. So, I nailed a 2X2 across the corner of the garage for them to roost on. I had to put them on it a few times before they figured that that is where they were supposed to sleep. It was working really well for a while, then one day when dad was working on the car, he washed his parts in a fairly good size pan of gas. When he was finished, he pushed it out of the way...right under the chicken's roost.

The next morning, dad said the chickens got drunk when they were roosting and inhaled those gas fumes all night and fell in the gas and drowned. Yup!!!! Now this was a sad, sad day for Rugged-Knee and me. We gathered up those poor, dead, gas-soaked chickens and put them in a couple of coffins consisting of two brown paper bags, grabbed a shovel and headed for the corner of the field. Poor Rugged-Knee's eyes were leakin' all the way there. I made a couple crosses out of the "chicken shit stained" roost wood. I said a little prayer for them and told Rugged-Knee that they were in a much nicer chicken coop in the sky. He was OK with that and we were back to normal in about 30 minutes.

Yup!!! Good times.

Back in the day when I was a kid, you learned a lot of stuff by trial and error. I think I had more errors than anyone else, but I think it helped my judgment a lot. I knew when to run. When you live out in the country and there are no streetlights or car lights at night you learn to appreciate stuff. Like the Milky Way, and the noises you can hear that no one else hears, like the frogs croakin' and the crickets cricketin'. Snakes don't say anything but scare the crap out of ya anyway. One thing I figured out when I was pretty young...the fields in the spring were jam packed with toads.

I always heard the frogs croakin' and would dig and dig for a flashlight that worked. I finally got one to work and went frog huntin'. Yup!! I had my flashlight and coffee can out in grandma's field where all the racket was comin' from. Now the problem with these frogs was, when ya get close, they shut up. So you stop moving, turn your light off and wait. When they start up again, you take one step, light out, and wait. Now all this racket was comin' from a brown toad about the size of a 50-cent piece and shaped the same. If you take a Kennedy half dollar, take Kennedy's face off and put on a toad's face, you have one. So, I found a couple of these guys and took them home. Now my mom already knows stuff. I am just learnin' stuff and fixin' to teach Rugged-Knee stuff. The next morning, I am outside sittin' on some old tires out on the sunny side of the garage, playin' with my new toys. I found out that they are perfectly comfortable lying flat on their back in the palm of your hand. I also found out that they like it if you rub under their chin and they also will pee full length of you if you poke them in the belly. Now these guys are pretty stinkin' cool. I can't wait to show Rugged-Knee. So, I have the other toad and head through the house, but I get stopped in the kitchen by Inspector #9. She wanted to know what I had and what I was going to do with it.

"Well, I was just goin' to, ummm, I just came to get..."

"Stanley, let me see what you have behind your back?" Now I know things aren't going well for me at this point, so if I want to save this toad's life, I better return him to my coffee can and have Rugged-Knee come out. Inspector #9 kinda helped me outside when she saw what it was. I was able to talk Rugged-Knee into comin' out and checkin' these guys out. I gave him the loaded one and I took the other. I showed him all the cool stuff they could do and said, "I wonder what he would do if you poked him in the belly?" Now one thing about Rugged-Knee is his curiosity gets the best of him and everything from then on is automatic. Yup!!!! Rugged-Knee shot himself right in the face. Now I don't have any idea why he started yellin'. I know it didn't hurt. I guess it's his way of gettin' even with me. I didn't even run, I just told mom the truth...that stinkin' toad peed in Rugged-Knee's face. They could whiz quite a ways!! Some kinda defense thing God gave them, I reckon.

Yup!!! Good Times.

***

I can remember when us kids got our very own beds. I was so excited that I didn't have to share with Rugged-Knee anymore. I really felt sorry for my mom because Rugged-Knee wasn't box trained yet. That was one reason I didn't like sleepin' with him. I remember getting up in the middle of the night quite often because the bed wasn't fit to sleep in anymore. I'd find the driest blanket on the bed and grab my pillow and curl up in the corner on the floor somewhere. He was only a couple years old, but mom thought he was old enough to sleep in my bed. Back in those days, the moms used cloth diapers. I don't care how big and thick the diaper was, Rugged-Knee could drench the thing. Mom used to have these plastic britches that she would put on him over the top of the cloth diaper. These were supposed to contain any mishaps. Sometimes that worked and sometimes it didn't. I remember playing in the bedroom with him once and I could smell somethin' that just wasn't right. I noticed the smell right after Rugged-Knee was sittin' there being really quiet, and not movin'. I sat there and watched him because it wasn't like him to not be screamin' or movin' much. He had this really weird look on his face when, well, there came the strangest sound I had ever heard in my whole 5 years of life!! It was pretty muffled, but I was pretty sure I knew what was goin' on. He wasn't foolin' me one bit. I knew it was a done deal when he started playin' and bouncin' around again like nothing happened. It sure didn't smell good in that bedroom. I got up to investigate. When I stepped around behind him, I saw a brown streak that went from the waist band of those plastic britches to the middle of his back. Rugged-Knee was so plump that the plastic britches fit pretty tight around his fat legs but there was so much pressure in there that it blew right up past the waist band. It's a good thing that they didn't make onesies back then. If they did, Rugged-Knee would have had twosies in his hair. No wonder he sat still till it was all over. If he had been in the wrong position, he could have flown around the room and broken my lamp or somethin'. Anyway, when I saw this, I had to break the news to mom. So she came and took him in the living room. When she took those rubber pants off and unpinned the diaper, this brown haze filled the living room and almost made me spew. I had to get out of there. This stuff will make ya sick! Didn't seem to bother Rugged-Knee or my Mom. She was as tough as they come. She filled the tub with water, took Rugged-Knee by the arms and dunked him in it like she was dunkin' a hard cookie in a cup of coffee. All his clothes went in the washer. After about an hour with all the doors and all the windows open, I could breathe again. Sure was a mess there for a while. We used to be pretty stinkin' tough back in those days.

Yup!!! Good Times.

***

It seems like ever since I can remember we have had a pet dog or cat. I think every cat we ever had was named either Spot or Fuzzy when I was pretty young, probably during my stinker years. I had this cat named Fuzzy and this cat followed me everywhere I went. I could be half a mile from home and good old Fuzzy would be right there. One day I was over at Mr. Sprinkle's field huntin'. Mr. Sprinkle had some 4' x 8' corrugated tin sheets laying out in his field that the wind blew out there...perfect huntin' tin. Now this was some of the best field mice huntin' this side of the Mississippi. Ya find a piece of tin, tippy toe up to it, slip your fingers under the edge of the tin and give it a flip so it turns over really quick. Most of the time there would be three or four mice under there. My dad said that cats were great hunters, but I think Fuzzy missed the memo. The first couple pieces of tin I flipped over, he just looked at me and the mice ran all around him. What a dork! So the next time I held him and when I flipped the tin over with one hand, I threw Fuzzy with the other. Thought for sure he would see the mice runnin' all over. Nope. He's just too stupid, so I'll catch them for him. Well, that went over like a screen door on a submarine...those little bastards bite! They only have four teeth, but those stinkin' teeth are huge. They are like a couple razor blades attached to a pair of pliers with eyes on both sides. Dangerous piece of equipment attached to a mouse. But I have my own piece of equipment. Yup!!! Rugged-Knee. We went over there with one of mom's quart canning jars and proceed to fill it up. We can keep the mice fresh for the cats if they are alive. I told Rugged-Knee to jump on the mouse when I flip the tin over. We'd get him by the nap of the neck and drop him in the bottle. Now I'm not sure which part Rugged-Knee didn't understand. When I flipped the tin over, Rugged-Knee did a swan dive from about six feet away and landed headfirst where I had just moved the tin. He had a long sleeve shirt on and when he was tryin' to gather himself up from his #9 Olympic dive, I saw a mouse run up the long sleeve of his shirt. I just stepped back thinkin', "This is going to be good." Well, Rugged-Knee didn't disappoint me one bit. He stood up and asked where the mouse went. So, I showed him the hole where he went in. I took his arm and held it straight up over his head and shook it, kinda like primin' a pump...worked pretty good. That's when that kid came unglued and freaked out. He started doing the Watusi, changed mid-stream to the Bossa Nova. Then the famous twist came in and he ended the performance with the Boogie Woogie. Pretty cool stuff. The field mouse came out the leg of his britches and beat feet through the grass. I'm not sure Rugged-Knee even knew he left. I couldn't get Rugged-Knee to help me catch mice ever again.

Yup!!! Good Times.

***

My dad used to take care of the betting machines at the horse races. Dad traveled all over, taking the equipment from Montana to Arizona, Idaho, Nevada, and Wyoming. One time, I remember us being in Mile City, Montana. I was around 13 years old at the time.

Rugged-Knee and I had had about enough horse racing for one day, so we went snoopin' around and found a field that had about half a dozen buffalo in it. It was almost like an arena with two big light poles about halfway across the field. Five of the buffalo were at one end. There was one by himself halfway between the other end and one of the light poles.

I was thinkin' pretty serious about sending Rugged-Knee runnin' across from one side of the field to the other to see what the single buffalo would do. But it was a little too dangerous for Rugged-Knee, so I'm thinkin' I'll give it a go. I had always out-run everything and everyone I had ever challenged before. So, I climbed over the fence. When I thought the buffalo wasn't lookin, I took off runnin' for the other side. About halfway to the light pole, I noticed the buffalo's tail up in the air. Now I have been around the block a few times and knew this wasn't a good sign. With the tail in the air, I got a glimpse of a pretty dang big pair of gonads. This is not a good sign of things to come. He dropped his head and started heading in my direction, kinda slow at first but pickin' up some steam. This isn't lookin' good for me. I weigh my chances, makin' decisions which seemed to change about every other step. I decide to head for the light pole. I throw my head back and run like I have never run before. I can hear some noise behind me. The sound of buffalo hooves pounding and Rugged-Knee yellin'. I'm pretty sure I was sayin', "Oh Shit, Oh shit!" all the way to the light pole. This big old buffalo is right on my tail as I stick my arm out to catch the light pole and swing around it. It amazed me this big fast buffalo could actually turn on a dime and give ya nine cents change! He was a lot faster than grandma's milk cow. I spun around the light pole thinking to do a 180, but he was still right there so we both ran around the light pole until I caught up to him. I had a vision at this point of grabbing his tail and bein' launched like a cracked whip towards the fence where Rugged-Knee was. I decided not to try that the second time around the pole, but instead made a runnin' break for it and headed for the fence. Rugged-Knee was jumpin' up and hollerin' down, "Run, Run, Run!!!" I had never run so fast in all my life. All I wanted to do was put real estate between that buffalo and me. I think I covered that 100 yards in 10 seconds flat. I didn't touch the ground or the top of the fence when I went over. I'm sure it was 6 feet high! I landed on the other side safe and sound. I looked to see where the buffalo was. He had stopped the second time around the light pole and was just watchin' all the action. Rugged-Knee was just getting even with me, I think.

Yup!!! Good Times.

We used to have cottontail bunnies close to our house when we lived near Three Forks, Montana. When I was around nine years old, I decided that I would like a few of these little critters closer to the house. Just seeing them out the window by chance wasn't enough. By golly if I wanted to see one, I wanted to see it any time I wanted. They are so stinkin' cute. The little, tiny baby bunnies are the cutest dang things, teeny spittin' images of their parents. There was a pile of wood posts and railroad ties across our lane near Mr. Sprinkle's circle drive. There was always a bunny there. So, I proceeded to get me one. I reckon it was like a candy store for me. I would see a bunny run into the pile of wood poles and by the time I dug down to him, he would run out the other end into a big batch of buffalo berry bushes. Well, these bunnies aren't dealing with a complete idiot here. I'm pretty stinkin' smart when it comes to figurin' out how to catch critters and get them home. I turned all the bottom poles around, so the fat end was closest to the bushes, which was about 50 feet away. Then I pulled the ends, so they were touching the pole next to it, so it kinda looked like a funnel and did the same thing with the railroad ties. There ya have it! I went home to make a peanut butter samich and wait. After a couple days I walked over there and sure enough, there was a bunny by the wood pile. I jumped up and down, yellin' and finally that cute little bunny ran right into my wood pile trap. Yes sir, just like I dreamed it. I started digging down through the wood and he was jammed up at the end of the poles and had no place to go. Aha!!! Gotchya!!! I reached down and got a hold of his ears so he couldn't get away, grabbed his rear end and slid him backwards so I could get to him. I got 'im!! He was so stinkin' cute! I held him up by his ears so I could check him out and he started kickin' and wigglin'. I thought that was how you were supposed to pick up a bunny…Elmer Fudd always did it to Bugs and he didn't kick and wiggle. Maybe that was because he was a wabbit? So, to calm him down, I held him like a cat and let go of his ears. I was just givin' him one of my loveable, softy hugs when that little bastard turned into a blender. I was trying to hold him up against my chest when those big-ass hind feet came into play. It was like trying to compress a coil spring against your chest. Little bunnies have toenails that are like lion claws. I wanted to see the expression on that little monster's face to see if he was scared or something, but he just leaned back so he could kick the crap out of me. I finally let go about halfway to the house and dropped the little creep. I didn't even give chase. When I lifted my shirt, my whole chest was scratched up. Be careful out there people. There are monsters in some pretty cute clothes.

Yup!!! Good Times.

***

When I was young, we had bunk beds because it was easier for more kids to sleep in one room. I shared a bedroom with my sister Lanette. We used to play "alligator" on the bed quite a bit. There were a bunch of kids on the top bunk and one guy on the bottom bunk. Someone on the top would dangle an arm or a leg over the side and the guy on the bottom had to grab them and hang on for a little while, 5 seconds or so. Then that guy had to be the alligator and you switched places.

It was fun until mom made us stop when I jerked my cousin Dean Cooper off the top bunk. I guess he wasn't expecting a big alligator. That ended the "alligator" game. Mom switched the bed for a trundle bed. You know, one bed lower than the other one with wheels on so it could roll under the other one. It was pretty cool, but I think my mom liked the bunk beds better because we couldn't jump up and down on either bed.

Rugged-Knee used to pull dirty tricks on me when I wasn't lookin'. He would do this when he knew I couldn't catch him before he made it to safety, hidden somewhere close to mom in the house. One day he threw a bucket of cold water on me when I was kneeling down tyin' my tennis shoes. By the time I caught my breath (you know the effect cold water has on ya) and finished my shoe, he had already cleared the corner of the house. I took pursuit, ran in the house, looked in the bedroom, under the bed and all over and couldn't find him. Sometimes mom would cover for the little creep. I figured maybe he had passed the door to the house and kept on runnin' so I went out to find him. As I walked past the bedroom window, I glanced in and that little creep came rolling out from under the bed lying on the bottom bed. He pulled the bottom bed out, got on it and rolled himself back under the upper bed using the springs to pull on. There were only about 8 inches between them. What a sneak! I kept it a secret and when he tried getting away after his next shenanigan, I gave him enough time to get in his hidey hole. Then I went runnin' in there and jumped up and down on the bed. Turns out, that little creep had gone into the bathroom instead! Mom gave me an ass chewin' for the bed jumping and since she was standin' in the doorway to the bedroom, I could not get out without collecting a few swats...almost knocked me off my feet a couple times. When my dad got home, I tried to talk him into putting in another door, one that led straight outside from my bedroom. I never did get one.

Yup!!! Good Times.

***

My little sidekick, Rugged-Knee, and I used to do some pretty fun stuff. I'm not really sure it was so fun for Rugged-Knee...he was always the one to quit, get hurt, or mad. It seemed like he would get mad, then get hurt, then quit. He just didn't have the drive it took to have a good time for a long time.

I remember watching TV one day with him, something about slow motion. It was the first time we had heard about slow motion and by cracky, it was pretty cool. So, we decided to have a bar room brawl...in slow motion. This seemed pretty cool, except most bar rooms don't have a couch and a big chair in them. So Rugged-Knee threw a left hook, caught me on the jaw and knocked me down onto the couch really slow. I gave him a punch in the stomach, and he doubled over and landed in the big chair, really slow. I slowly jumped on him and gave him a couple more to the chin. He tagged me with a right hook on the chin and I fell back on the couch. Then we wrestled around and stood up. That's when Rugged-Knee lost his cool. He evidently didn't like me getting the best of him in slow motion. So, he turned on the afterburners like he was wanting to play for keeps. He started throwing real punches. I mean if he had connected, he would have wrinkled my shirt. Now this is the problem Rugged-Knee had...if he couldn't hit me, he got madder! I didn't try to stop him from trying to hit me. Heck, that wouldn't be fair, so I let him swing away and just dodged the blows. This really pissed him off and now he was out for blood. I kept dodging him and he was getting madder and madder! Now he is just plain upset. He's going to rip my eyes out if he can just get me! He finally grabbed my shirt and now I have to do somethin'. I grabbed him by his arms like they do in the movies when the guy is facin' ya, falls backwards, puts his feet in the other guy's belly and throws him over his head with his feet. There must have been somethin' I didn't remember. It worked really good for the Lone Ranger. Anyway, the plan was to launch Rugged-Knee into the big chair. I tried, I really did, but it just wasn't meant to be I reckon. I launched him a little higher than I imagined the seat of the chair to be, but about 2 feet too far to the right. He ricocheted off the side of the chair and then back of the couch. I had a few sore spots by the time mom was finished showing me what parts Rugged-Knee could have hurt. I spent the rest of the evening in my bedroom by myself playing basketball with a balloon...in slow motion.

Yup!!! Good Times.

Dad was always changin' the house, movin' somethin' here or there. You know how women move the furniture around in the house? Not in our family...dad would leave the furniture and somehow move the room.

My aunt, uncle and cousins came up to visit one day. Us kids were outside playin' while the grown-ups were sittin' at the table drinkin' coffee and talkin'. We have a bathroom inside and one outside. My cousin Dean always waited till the very last minute to head for the toilet. I just didn't understand why he waited so long. Every time, it was a desperation run for the toilet and a "must go right now" situation. This is what I call misery...Dean dancin' around and hangin' onto stuff, so he doesn't have an accident. Now these kids are from the city and don't know nothin. They live in Manhattan and I bet maybe 1,500 people live there. But, if I'm outside playing and have to whiz, I just sidestep a couple feet, cut loose and then go back to what I was doin'. That's how I learned to write my name in the snow! Sometimes I could only spell Stan and not Stanley. Pretty sure it's OK as long as you're not too close to the house. We still had the old 2 holer out back so if push came to shove and there was a girl around, you could always run out behind that old toilet...probably even go inside it if ya had to.

Well, anyway, Dean dances his way to the house instead of behind somethin' like I told him...there is a toilet behind every bush, tall weed, tractor or truck. I remember whizzin' once on the far side of mom's car when she came out and got in to head to town. It was quite a chore to keep up with the car when she backed out and keep from whizzin on myself. It was kinda like trollin'. Oh yeah, so Dean gets to the house and runs inside to go in the bathroom. He forgot that dad and uncle George had changed the door to the bathroom to the other wall and had sealed the old doorway shut. It was kinda dark in that little hallway and Dean ran into the new wall, landed on the floor and peed his pants. I could hear the ass-chewin' he was receivin' from outside. It sounded pretty cool 'cause it wasn't directed at me for once. I just sat outside and enjoyed the yellin'. Wasn't long before Dean came back out wearin' a pair of my britches. Picked up where we left off.

Yup!!! Good Times.

***

I remember when we received our first telephone. It was yellow and had a little circle with 4 numbers on the front. It just hung on the wall with a receiver on it and that was it. If we wanted to call someone, we picked up the receiver and put it to our ear. An operator said, "Number please." We would tell her the four-digit number and she would hook us up with the person we wanted to call. Pretty stinkin' cool. We were on a party line, which means there are others on the same line, and you could hear them talk to someone else. It was an honor system back then. Everyone could be trusted (almost).

We were the last on our party line... Joneses, Goldburgs and Callantines. The Joneses were old folks and first on our line. When the phone rang once, it was their call, and we didn't answer the phone. Then came the Goldburgs who lived between town and our house. They had a teenage boy and a daughter about four years older than my sister. Her name was Louise, and she was a fox. When the phone rang twice, it was their call. Our call was two quick rings, a space and two quick rings again. That was pretty cool stuff. I remember everyone racing to get to the phone when it rang, excited to talk with someone besides our family...even though it was always for my sister and we knew it. I had to get a chair to stand on to reach the phone and would get knocked off when everyone else showed up to answer the phone. I never ever got to answer it, so when someone answered it, I would yell from afar "HELLO!!!!". I always had to be prepared to run because my sister would slap me around until she ran out of phone cord. We had a cord on our receiver that would allow my sister to take it into her bedroom. I used to click the little do-dad on the wall phone up and down once in a while when she was in the middle of a conversation. Holy Smoke! She would come flyin' out of the bedroom! I still don't understand why she thought she had to maim someone to let them know she didn't like what they did. My mom was lucky she had a really tough son that could take a beatin.

Now even though I was only in 2nd grade, and our neighbor Louise Goldburg was in the 8th, I could tell she was... nicely put together. I used to just stare at her, kinda in a trance. It was like she was radiant, and the light just glowed off of her white hair. One time I was listenin' to Louise Goldburg talkin' to a boy for about 30 seconds, and right in the middle of a sentence, she said, "Stanley I know you are on here."

I said, "No I'm not."

Next day on the bus, Louise gave me one of those mean looks. You know what I'm talkin about...the ones big sisters give little brothers. I could also tell at school who my sister was talkin' about because her friends would give me that brotherly love look too. Girls didn't like me much...called me a "nuisance"!

Yup!!! Good Times.

***

One Christmas I remember getting my very own radio alarm clock. Now these were the coolest dang things. Rugged-Knee received one as well. Mine was tan and his was white, but mine was a little classier, which made me feel really good because I always thought mom loved Rugged-Knee more than me. Since I received the super neat lookin' one, I now know I'm right up there with Rugged-Knee. Yup!!! Getting the crap slapped out of me, on average every other day, means she loves me, yes sir! (On that note, I'm pretty sure my wife loves me too.) Well, these things even had a snooze on them. Mom said if I pushed that button on top, I could sleep for three minutes before the alarm would go off again. Well, that didn't make sense. Why would I want to wake up to shut the alarm off so I could sleep three more minutes? Gosh, if I'm goin' to wake up with the alarm, I might as well stay up, so I don't get mad when the alarm goes off the second time. That would wreck my whole day.

I've heard some words come from my sister's room when her alarm went off for the second time that would have gotten me in big trouble. I think she even throws stuff. So, I get my alarm clock all set to wake me up at 7:00 Saturday mornin'. Oh, one more thing. My radio alarm clock has a timer on it...yes, it does. There is a little knob on the face of the clock that you turn and the radio plays for up to 1 hour. It worked like the timer my mom had sittin' on the back of the stove. Yup!!! I would crank that to one hour and lay there listening to "KOMA fm radio Oklahoma City". I always cranked it up a little, making it hard to go to sleep, but I had great music to listen to. It never failed. Right in the middle of the best song ever, that dang thing would shut off. I'd have to get up and set it to play again. Good grief, now I'm awake, laying there listening to more great songs for a while. Finally, morning comes, and I wake up at about 8:30. That stupid alarm clock doesn't work. Oh yeah...AM and PM! OK, I've got this. So, Saturday night I have it all set to go off for Sunday morning. I listen to some more great music Saturday night but, Sunday morning, that dang alarm didn't go off again. Now what? Oh, this alarm clock wakes you up with the radio, but we can't get KOMA in the daytime, only at night. If you fall asleep with the radio on, you wake up in the mornin' to a buzzin' sound. Well, that doesn't make sense. The heck with that silly alarm clock. Mom always got me up before, and I like my music.

Yup!!! Good Times.

***

One day, my dad poured a 6' X 10' slab of cement right behind our house. Then he built a big 4' X 4' wooden box on it with a four foot lid. With that big lid and all, I was thinkin' it would be a great place for critters I caught. I could put a mess of them in there I betcha!

If I could find our Fuzzy cat, I'd see how it works. He is hiding from me again. If I fire up the vacuum cleaner and run it around the places he hides, he runs out and heads for the great out-of-doors. He doesn't like the vacuum 'cause I put it right on him. He always comes in the house full of weeds, so I started suckin' it off him. He didn't mind at first, but kinda objected when I sucked his tail up in there. If ya stick the hose on his nose it takes his breath away. You can turn a switch on the vacuum and make it blow instead of suck. Once, I thought I had sucked all the air out of Fuzzy, so I put it on blow and shoved that on his nose. He didn't like that, I guess. He always tried to put some real estate between me and him. Fuzzy's tail was longer than most cats, and since his tail was always the last to leave, I latched on to it. I wasn't stretchin' it...he was doin' the pullin'. I don't know about other cats, but Fuzzy sure had claws that cat tore up a few couches, chairs, and at least one little kid that I know of. So, I never could pitch Fuzzy in Dad's box. He must have always been outside hidin'.

It took me about a month to figure out what that box was all about. One day some guys came out and spent the whole day hangin' around dad's big wooden box. I didn't think much about it, I had stuff to do in the woods. When I came home, they were all gone. But now, in four different places around our house, there were big round outlet lookin' things with a shiny chrome cap with a hinge on one side. When you lifted the cap, a vacuum fired up and sucked like crazy. It was the coolest thing! All mom had was a hose...no vacuum cleaner machine to push around. This was the strongest vacuum suction I had ever seen. Well, I guess it was only the second vacuum I'd ever seen, but this thing could really suck! I'm lookin all over for Fuzzy to try this thing out, but mom told me never to stick that hose on Fuzzy. I think she was afraid if I did, I might turn him inside out.

OK, so now I wonder where Rugged-Knee is. I'm thinkin' if I could back him up against one of those doors and get that door open, he wouldn't be able to run anywhere. That big box that dad built is where all the stuff mom vacuumed up went. I know that's where stuff went because I kinda sucked up some things I got slapped around for...Rugged-Knees socks, my sister's underwear, my little John Deer tractor, oh yeah, and Rugged-Knee's oatmeal, and some other stuff. But they are just out in that box.

Yup!!! Good Times.

***

I don't remember very many Christmases when I was growing up. It's probably because we didn't have much, but I do remember one year my parents got each one of us kids something cool. I have no idea where they got the money, but I bet it cost them about $75.00. My sister received a new doll and one of those little cook stoves that she could cook real cake mixes in. The doll was pretty cool, its name was Bonnie Braids. When you laid her down on her back, she closed her eyes and went to sleep. My sister still has Bonnie. On the other hand, I have no idea where the stove went.

I can tell you that when my sister's eyes were closed, it didn't mean she was asleep. She had a lot of those little cake mixes and only shared a little tiny piece with me. It only took 5 minutes for one of those little cakes to bake in her oven. One day she was taking a nap (I thought) and left a little cake mix on the table. I was quite the cook back then, so I added water to the mix in a little bowl and mixed 'er up. They had no instructions on the box telling how to cook it, but the little oven, which was in her closet, did. I knew if I took that thing out of her closet, I'd be in trouble, so I found a small extension cord to hook up. I poured the cake mix in her little pan and crawled across her bedroom floor to the closet and started cookin' that cake. As I sat there under her clothes waiting for it to get done, it started to smell pretty stinkin' good. Then my sister's closet exploded. Shoes were flyin', clothes were flyin', choice words were flyin'! I was scramblin' on my hands and knees tryin' to get a dress off me while gettin' a beatin' with a belt. I think she had that belt under her pillow just in case her little brother snuck into her room. With the belt doubled over, she whipped me like a racehorse. I was now on my belly scratchin' the floor tryin to make it just a couple more feet. She wouldn't stop hammerin' on me until mom got between us to break it up. Lanette always had to have the last word, capping it off with a kick or a slap...just to make sure she got her point across. By this time, the cake is done. My sister pulled that dress off me and went back to her room. She put all her stuff back in her closet and was sitting on the bed eating the cake I made for her. Sometimes she just didn't appreciate the good things I did for her. Heck, I baked her a cake and got her to do a little workout as well.

Yup!!! Good Times.

***

Back in the 1950's and 1960's, there was a game the girls used to play called "Jacks". I never did see the sense in the game and just never understood the rules and scoring. There were a bunch of little game pieces that looked like space stations, each with two ends that came to a sharp point at each end. They were about ½ inch from one tip to the other, then there were four arms that came off the middle in each direction with a little ball on the ends also. Then there was a separate little rubber ball to top the game off. Now I don't know what all the rules were, but the girls would sit on the sidewalk and throw all the jacks down. Then they would bounce the ball, grab a jack and catch the ball before it landed. I think each time they did that, they grabbed more jacks. When they missed the ball or a jack, it was another girls' turn. I watched this a couple times from afar, trying to figure it out. I was afraid of girls, so I didn't dare ask. Heck, they might think I was stupid or somethin', or might even want me to play. It just didn't make much sense to me. I would have slammed that ball down pretty hard, grabbed all the jacks and caught the ball. "Game over."

So my sister had a "Jacks" game and carried it around with her everywhere. One day she kinda forgot to take them to her room, and Stanley saw them. I didn't think it was a big deal to mess with 'em a little. Sooo, I was dinkin' around with them on the kitchen table, seein' how many jacks I could get spinnin' like a top before the first one fell. Unfortunately, I was so involved in my game that my sister caught me. I don't know why she couldn't just say somethin' instead of sneakin' up behind me and slapping me off the chair before she saying a word. She had me on the floor and changed tactics. Then, every time her elbow bent, her mouth flew open. The foot came into play and the knee now made the mouth fly open. I was tryin' to get off the floor from behind the table. She would kick and when I popped up, she slapped me. Every time she slapped me, my head hit the wall...kinda like those fair games, "bop-a-gopher" or somethin'. To save myself I fell to the floor under the table and scrambled to the far side where the mad cow disease wasn't present. She was yelling at me for "stringin' her stinkin' jacks all over the place". I did not do that. They were all on the table when I left. A couple days or so after this incident, I laid on a jack in my bed and that sumbitch hurt. I put that jack back so she wouldn't catch me. The next morning, I got out of bed and stepped on one with my bare feet. That sumbitch hurt too. I put that one back as well. I'm pretty dang sneaky, but I don't know where the stinkin' jacks were comin' from. I didn't take any! The next day I found one in my shoe when I put it on. That's when I started my own "Jacks" collection. She was pretty mean! Sisters are like that sometimes.

Yup!!! Good Times.

***

I was a busy guy when I was young and I usually had somethin' to do. If I didn't have anything planned, I'd sit in my favorite thinkin' spot on the east side of the garage facing town. I would go out there in the mornin' about 9:00 when it was quiet out. Dad had some old tires leaning up against the garage almost all the way to the end of the garage. About 9:00 or 9:30 in the morning, they would be warm from the mornin' sun, just right for sittin and thinkin'.

One Saturday in the spring I was out enjoyin' the birds singin'. It had rained the evening before, so the air was nice and fresh. I was just enjoyin' life and tryin' to figure out what to do that day. I was deep in thought when I heard the door to the house fly open and Rugged-Knee yellin', "SICK-EM, SICK-EM, GET-EM." Our cat Fuzzy came flyin' around the side of the garage headed for the center of the tires I was sittin' on. Then came my dog Herman, an Australian Shepherd who had no dignity what-so-ever. He went after Fuzzy like they were hooked together with an invisible rope about 6 feet long. I tried to get off before Fuzzy dove through the tires. Herman followed like a bull in a china closet. As they came my way, it started a domino effect, and before I knew it I was layin' on the ground. The tires were full of water from rain the night before, so when the cat came out, he was like a wet mop and didn't miss a lick when he went over me, stringing water everywhere. When I was tryin' to get up, I glanced down to see what damage the cat did to my belly. That's when Herman broke through the end of the tires, totally focused on the cat, and knocked me head-over-tin-cup. Now there is no smell like a wet Herman. He loves rolling in dead skunks, and cow pies and he didn't seem to care if they were old or fresh. That was one thing about Herman...you could smell him before you saw him. At this point I didn't know whether to stay down or make a break for it. Then the culprit of the whole thing...Rugged-Knee, came around the corner still yellin' "SICK-EM" as he ran past me. He was focused on Herman, tryin' to keep up as he passed me in the dirt. Rugged-Knee could always get Herman fired up over the cat.   Last I saw, all three were headed for the shed out back. Dang kids anyway! Ya know, I don't even remember what I ended up doing that day.

Yup!!! Good Times.

***

When I was young, I would do anything for anyone. I used to get kinda bored whenever we went to my grandparents' house and none of my cousins were there. I think both of my grandpas liked it that way, though. I was the good little kid, when I didn't have anyone to get into trouble with. My grandpa Thompson had a big crosscut saw that hung on the back of his garage. He had sawhorses out there and I would go out and cut his wood for him with a saw that was two feet longer than I was tall. My grandpa Callantine had a big pile of wood that always needed to be split with an ax, so I would split his wood for him. For being only 10 years old, I was pretty good at cutting wood. I would split it all day long. I was splitting wood one day at Grandpa Callantine's when I saw the tall weeds next to the barn movin'. Me being me, I decided to check it out. Now I don't just go around lookin' for trouble but somehow it finds me. There in those tall weeds was a hen and about a dozen little yellow chicks. Everywhere the hen went, the chicks went with her, every step. I sure wanted to hold one of those little chicks. I tried to scatter the chicks so I could get one. Did you know that chickens are mean little sumbitches? But this one takes the cake! She had more kids than she knew what to do with...so why would she miss one for a few minutes? But no, this hen had an attitude. I didn't even touch that little yellow chick and she was all over me like a cat on a hot tin roof. That chicken was peckin' me and flogging me with her wing, kickin' the crap out of me. You would think I had stepped on a beehive! I tried hard to get out of Dodge, and put some real estate between us, but she kept after me. I tried running through the garden, but she jumped out of the cabbages. I headed for the corn and down a row or two, but she met me by the beans. I ran through the raspberries headed for the lawn and she was with me all the way. I finally lost her when I jumped into the canal. I think the only reason she didn't come after me was because she couldn't swim. Ever since then, I have always wondered why us guys call girls "Chicks."

Yup!!! Good Times.

***

I really don't remember how old I was around 12 I suppose...we used to have an old 1936 Chevy PU truck us kids would drive around the field in. Once in a while we would drive it over to the river to go fishin'. At first, I didn't drive it a lot because it had a little lever on the gear shifter that I couldn't figure out. But once I figured it out, heck I was in that old truck until it would run out of gas. The little lever was a lock out for reverse gear, so you didn't accidently go from a forward gear into reverse. This was the coolest old truck west of the Mississippi river. Sometimes when you were shifting it, the gear shifter would pop off the column and it looked like you were left holding grandma's cane. So, you'd have to stop and stick it back down in the hole it came out of and turn the little piece that was supposed to keep it in there. It would work great for about 20 times and come out again. One day we were going over to the beaver pond by the river to do a little fishin', and Ed was driving. We got there, just started fishin' and Ed catches a real nice German Brown trout...about 3lbs. He got it to shore and took off runnin for the truck. I heard the truck start and head out. Seems he is goin home, left me sittin there and he's headed for the house. But luck would be with me because he had to stop at the gate and open it about 150 yards away. It's about 3 miles to the house, so I grabbed my fishin' pole and started runnin'. I got to the gate about the time he gets it closed and I throw my pole over the fence and into the truck. Now I need to get my tail in there before he leaves me again. I climbed through the gate and over the truck's tailgate into the back as the gravel flies up behind the tires of the old Chevy and we are off. We had to cross the highway to get to our house and Ed headed across with a California stop.

When he went into second gear...he missed and hit reverse. The tires squealed and went back to where the stop sign was that we just came from. I guess he was supposed to stop and do it right. Gotta come to a complete stop and then we can go. That stupid fish is still hooked onto his pole when we get to the house. Well, I guess we were done fishing. Ed has his fish and I have my pole (I am so stinkin' lucky). Ed was always like that. "I got mine, you're on your own."

Yup!!! Good Times.

***

I really wanted a treehouse when I was little, but the only trees were over at Mr. Sprinkle's property or in the woods 3/4 of a mile away. So, my kick in the side, Rugged-Knee and I started packin' stuff over to the woods. I found a great big cottonwood tree that had the perfect branches and they kinda hung out over the river a bit...a pretty cool place for a treehouse. We packed a lot of boards, tools and a rope over there. We tied the rope around Rugged-Knee's waist and up over a branch. When he had a bit of a load tied to one end, he would run as fast as he could to some branches on a nearby tree, grab them and hang on. That gave me enough time to pull them to me. We had planned our floor plan to stick out over the water a little bit. This was going to be our porch and we had visions of sittin' on the porch fishin' all day.

Ya know, sometimes things just don't go the way you planned. I got down to help Rugged-Knee tie on a couple heavier boards. I made sure he could pull the weight of the boards before I climbed back up to the floor suspended over the water. He was good with the plan, but depended on the other tree branches holding him until I got those boards unloaded on that upper floor. It is very important to have the load straight under the point where the rope goes over the branch. When Rugged-Knee took off and the wood came off the ground, they both swung out over the river. Now this wasn't expected and put on a little extra force. Rugged-Knee tried to grab the branches long enough for me to grab the wood, but the branches broke just as I reached for it. That jerked me enough to break the branches that the porch was relying on which then sent me into a jack knife dive into the river. Now this then launched Rugged-Knee up off the ground about 7 feet or so and when I looked up from my dive, he was swingin' back and forth over the water. I hollered for him to plug his nose. I would need to let the boards go and then he could drop safely into the water. Yup!!...That was the plan. So I let go of the wood which came up faster than I had anticipated! It snagged my t-shirt, caught me in the chin and knocked me silly for a minute.

Unfortunately, things didn't go so well with Rugged-Knee either. He had his nose plugged with one hand and his other arm stretched out like he was going to do a one arm dive, but it turned into a belly flop into water that was only about 4 inches deep. This is the only time I can remember hearing someone say words underwater and I could understand them. Boy, what a whiny baby with a lot of foul words. Rugged-Knee left me there sittin' in my dreams all soaking wet, kinda put a damper on things. He didn't even take any tools home when he left.

I just never understood why he let little things like that wreck the day.

Yup!!! Good Times.

***

Acts of nature sometimes are so brutal that I just don't see how Rugged-Knee and I managed to grow up.

I don't remember how old Rugged-Knee was when this transformation started to take place...around 7, I reckon. I don't think he was ready for it. I, on the other hand, had already gone through this and didn't think it was that big of a deal. My goodness! Rugged-Knee thought the world was coming to an end and really put up a struggle to keep the inevitable from occurring. Yup!!

That loose tooth was comin' out. That little creep whined about his loose tooth for weeks. Mom gave him everything good to eat just to keep him quiet. She fed him cream of wheat cereal, whipped cream, jello, and even mashed his bananas. His time was comin', though. I tried to trick him into letting me help get rid of that stinkin' loose tooth. If I could just get a string around it. I tried sweet talkin' him and tried to trade stuff, like my best marbles, or my frog swatter, but I just couldn't convince him to let me help.

We were outside on the steps when he agreed to let me tie some string around it by promising that the pressure would ease that tooth right up out of there. Yup!!! And he wouldn't even know until it came out and left a hole where it used to be. So I told him to stay right there while I went out to the shed to get some string.

Now Herman, our dog, did two things very well. If I told him to stay, he would stay right there even if he couldn't see me. So, I had him sit just around the corner of the house. I tied one end of the string around his collar and dragged the string on the ground to Rugged-Knee and tied the other end around his tooth. The second thing Herman did really good was retrievin' a ball that was thrown past the corner of the house. Yup!!! No other dog could hold a candle to Herman's retrievin' skills. Once that ball left my hand, removing Rugged-Knee's tooth was a done deal.

I don't know why he was so upset! Maybe he thought he could get 10 cents for it from the tooth fairy, but the tooth was somewhere between the house and the outdoor toilet behind the house. Or...maybe because I tricked him... or because his mashed banana days were over.

Good old Herman. What a doggie! I called him Dr. Herman for a couple days.

Yup!!! Good Times.

***

Sometimes you learn valuable lessons, even when you are pretty young. Now my sister, Lanette, taught me stuff when I was younger that I still use today. She taught me how to protect myself and how to get away from her when I did things she didn't agree with. I used to be able to run 100 yards in 10 seconds flat. That was something my sister couldn't do. She also taught me that if it is not yours, leave it the hell alone.

She had this do-dad called a hula-hoop. I watched the girls play with them at school. I was pretty sure I could operate one just as well as the girls did. There was one right there behind the couch. Yup!!

"Hey Rugged-Knee, watch this!" I had no idea where she had come from and can't help but wonder if I had a target on the back of my head since that was the direct point of impact my sister always aimed for. Couch cushions knock you off your feet when you are not expecting their company. When you have connected with a cushion at supersonic speed from behind, it's pretty hard to stay in your shoes. I went skiddin' across the living room floor and my tennis shoe passed me up. She drew that cushion back again, smashed it down on my head and I almost banged my face on the floor. (She had her stupid hula-hoop, so I didn't see a problem at this point.) As usual, she still hadn't said anything. As she started to draw that cushion back again, I grabbed her pedal pushers and was tryin' to pull them down so she couldn't run. (Another thing she taught me was how to use time effectively.) I reckon I should have been runnin'. I was able to get control of my feet and was finally runnin' for the door when her female brain kicked into throwin' mode. She pitched that cushion and knocked me silly up against the door. As I tried to come to my senses, she was all over me kickin' and scratchin'. As I finally broke free, she grabbed my shirt...I felt like I was caught in a blender!

I was outside examinin' myself for damage control when Rugged-Knee stepped out eatin' an apple, looked at me all calm like and said, "That was pretty cool Damley !!!"

Yup!!! Good Times.

***

When you grow up in the country, you learn a lot of stuff about life on your own. There used to be a pond about half a mile from our house where I used to play all the time. My biggest problem was mom's rule..."Don't get wet". How can a kid that lives in the country honor such a request? I tried my hardest, but when your little brother, Rugged-Knee, slipped and got wet, it was ok because he did it first, right? When he isn't around and you are by yourself, then what? I was doing the frog thing 'cause it was spring and all the little frogs were sittin' on the moss just far enough away you couldn't reach them. When you tried, they jumped in the water, not to be seen till the next trip around the pond.

There was a big frog I had my sights on hiding in the cattails... I really wanted him, but I had to honor my mom's rule. Usually, I cut myself a green cattail about 3 feet long to bop frogs on the head. Pretty cool. You smacked them and all four legs would fly out. I would keep my toes on the edge of the pond, put one hand in the water, stretch out over the water and give them a bop. Then I worked my way back to shore and fished them out with a willow. I stayed dry and had a frog to boot. Well, this frog was out almost as far as I could stretch. I stretched out and got ready to whap him on the head when I heard this swishin' sound. It went away. I heard it again and, as I twisted my body to look up, this black bird hit the back of my head and knocked me ass-over-tin-cup into the mossy water. As I started to get up, he came at me again. I was a mess, covered in green slimy moss! That stinkin' bird was a mean sumbitch with a nasty attitude. I finally got far enough away from the cattails that he left me alone.

If I go home now, I might be in trouble, so I spent the rest of the day in the willows in my shorts with my shirt and pants hangin' over a few limbs dryin'. When I got home, all dried out, Mom asked me if I was savin' the moss in my pockets and ears for somethin' special.

Sometimes you wish your little brother was with you to experience the good stuff.

Yup!!!!!! Good Times

***

I had so much fun with my little brother Rugged-Knee that at times I forgot I had another brother. Ed was older by a year, but we didn't do much together, not like Rugged-Knee and I did. I received a bicycle for Christmas one year and when spring sprung, Ed decided he needed one because I had too much fun on mine. He bought one just like mine, but mine was faster than his. I talked him into going for a ride with me one day down the back road...what I called "around the block". It was about five miles all together. It would be great bonding time for me and Mr. Ed.

We had tried this once before. A bull snake crossed the road as we were racing to a crossroad. I was winnin' the race and I yelled, "Snake!" Mr. Ed rides by with his feet on the handlebars so the snake can't get him and yells over his shoulder, "You stay there! I'm goin' to get mom." My older brother was such a pansy!

Well, I'm willin' to give it another try and see if we can't spend some good time together. Things are goin' pretty good and we only have about a mile and a half to go. It's been a great day. We are headed down this lane that normally has some bees on the other side of some Buffalo Berry bushes not too far from the road. I always move to the far side of the road and ride on like they weren't there. Mr. Ed, on the other hand, is scared of stuff. He yells at me to ride really fast thinking he can ride faster than the bees can fly. I tried that once, it doesn't work! Before I could warn him, he is kinda teasin' them, yellin' stuff like "They can't catch us!" as he rides past me. Mr. Ed's yelling turned into screamin' about 30 feet past me. I saw a line of bees chasin' him. I don't think I could have beat him in a race at that moment.

By the time I got to the house Ed couldn't see out of his right eye. Mom had him by the kitchen sink checkin' him out. The screamin' must have started when a bee stung him on the back, probably about the point where I saw his bike get so wobbly, I thought he was goin' to shake it apart. He also got stung on the right cheek and it had swollen up like a grapefruit. That must have been when his bike got away from him, shot across the road, down into the ditch and back up on the road again. I thought Mr. Ed was going to ditch the bike! He hadn't missed a beat pumpin' at high speed and screamin'. He must have needed that air flow for his afterburners. Pretty stinkin' cool. I'd go with Mr. Ed again, but if I remember right, Mr. Ed didn't want much to do with me after that.

Yup!!! Good Times.

∗∗∗

When I was little, I had hundreds of pets.

Every spring I'd get new ones. All kinds of birds would give me one or two of their little ones to raise. I'm not sure they knew they were givin' them to me, a lot of them sure bitched about it. I let them have their share of the kids. I kept most of the birds in my chicken coop, a 1949 Plymouth coupe with the windows rolled down a little. Had all the seats covered with cardboard because of the white stuff which my dad said was bird poop. I never questioned what my dad told me; he was a pretty smart man. So anyway, it sure was a chore to get all that cardboard cut just right and put in place since they didn't have duct tape back then. I wound up foldin' it and tuckin' it in here and there. I finally got it all covered so the seats didn't get wrecked. I think it would have been easier if I had weaved a 10' X 20' shack out of willows. But this thing had windows in it and would hold about 50 Magpies, 25 Redwing Blackbirds and 10 Mourning Doves all at once.

The gophers, bunnies, and skunks had to share dad's shed out behind the house. I would catch all these guys when they were little, raise them and turn them loose. For some reason I thought I could do a better job than their parents.

I caught my first pet and took him home when I was about eight. I had so much trouble with him I almost didn't get any more pets. He liked to eat dandelions and pansy flowers. He used to get me in all kinds of trouble with my mom and I was always lookin' for him. He would be in one place one minute and if I turned my back, he would disappear, and I'd spend a while lookin' for him. I named him FLASH. I had him for a couple days before mom convinced me to turn my turtle Flash loose back where I got him, in the pond across the lane.

Yup!!! Good Times.

***

When I was little, mom couldn't afford to buy me gloves so I wore socks on my hands to play in the snow. You couldn't hold much with them, but you could run and roll a snowball to make a snowman. On the other hand, when my little brother was 5, mom got him mittens. We called them 'idiot mittens'. These mittens had a looong string sewn to the cuff of each mitten. Mom stuffed the string up one sleeve and down the other sleeve. When the kid held both arms out (with the mittens on), the string went from the tip of one middle finger all the way across his shoulders to the middle finger of the other hand. When Rugged-Knee took his coat off, the mittens stayed with his coat. Pretty stinkin' cool, huh??

Somebody figured out that you could run up to him, jerk his right mitten off pretty hard when he wasn't expectin' it, and he would hit himself in the head with his left hand. Kinda like a string puppet. I got in trouble quite a few times back then. :) Yup!!! Good Times.

***

Sometimes when you are really little, there are things that scare you and there are things that should scare you, but you don't know any better. Chickens for instance.

I reckon I was five or six years old and had a big wart on my finger. That old wart was red like a cherry and seemed like it was the size of a tootsie pop. Whenever I put my hand in my pocket or bumped it on somethin', it would bleed pretty bad. Mom made a doctor appointment over in Butte to have it removed.

Mom decided to stop over at my grandma's ranch on the way to Butte to visit for a while. I was outside playin' with my cousin Judy. We played on the trunk of a big Cottonwood tree that grandpa and dad had cut down. Grandma let most of her chickens run loose. We would try to catch one and go sit on the tree and hold it. I caught a Road Island Red, I think. Hilda was a mighty fine chicken, really nice...until she took a shine to my wart. That hen pecked it a couple times and it started to bleed. I let go of Hilda...I thought she wanted loose, but she wanted a piece of me. She chased me all over that stinkin' barnyard. I ran past the chicken coop, past the pig pen, in one door of the barn and out the other. That chicken ran like the wind! I lost her somewhere around the milkin' stalls.

I tried to sneak around the barn back to my cousin, but that chicken came from nowhere! I felt somethin' run straight up my back, doin' the watusi on the back of my head. I started to run, tripped over some chicken wire on the ground and fell face first in the dirt. Big Red was all over that wart like a virus in my computer. My good old cousin ran interference for me while I gathered myself up. I shook the dirt, chicken poop and feathers out of my suspenders and britches as I headed for the house. Grandma said that chickens love ladybugs and was pretty sure Hilda figured she got the cream of the crop. I think my mom thanked God for that chicken!

It was sure exciting, just as scary as the doctor and cheaper as well. It's one thing to hold a Big Red Chicken, but it's another thing when the chicken wants you for lunch. I'm sure glad that blood thirsty chicken didn't have teeth!

Yup!!! Good Times.

***

When I was about 4 or 5 years old, we were over at my grandparents' ranch for supper one evening, no special occasion, just a get together. There was no TV back then, but there was plenty of entertainment.

Granny had a big kitchen with a wood burning stove in it. There was a big butcher block right in the middle of her kitchen. For a little kid like me, this thing was huge, about 5-foot square. It seemed like everyone else was doin' somethin'...Grandpa chuckin' wood in the stove, my mom doin' somethin' at the sink and dad just teasin' everyone. I couldn't see the top of the butcher block without grabbing the edge of it, standing on my tip toes and peekin' over the edge. Granny had a great big butcher knife for cutting up chicken. She was wavin' this big old knife around like it was nothin' and chicken parts were flyin'. I think my dad was tossin' them over to the sink to my mom. While I was peekin' over the edge of the butcher block, that big old knife came crashin' down and a chicken leg shot off the block. Grandma looked me right in the eyes and said, "Son, if you don't back away from my block, I'll skin you alive." Yup, skeered the heck out of me and I ran for the barn, way past the chicken coop.

I thought granny had been pretty ornery, but I came back, and watched from the kitchen doorway... you know, in case granny was serious about me being in her kitchen!

Dad was standing at the butcher block holding a great big pickle in front of granny's face, teasin' her with it. When granny went to take a bite, dad would jerk it away. Well, just as dad stuck the pickle in front of her, she chomped down and when dad pulled the pickle back...granny's teeth were still embedded in the pickle!!! Just hangin' on for dear life!! I'm sure my eyes bugged out! What the heck?? I blinked a time or two, but those teeth were still in that pickle. I'll never forget the look on grandma's face, kinda looked like a football with no air in it wearin' glasses. Granny and everyone started laughin'! She grabbed her teeth which were still attached to the pickle and headed for the bathroom. When she came out, she had her face back.

That was when I first saw my real granny.

Yup!!! Good Times.

***

When I was around six years old, we didn't always have much money for clothes and things we needed, but somehow my mama got us by. Mama insisted on a few things I didn't like but had to use. One of these was a pair of suspenders to hold my britches up. My sister thought they were for a few other uses. She would sneak up from behind, pull them back and turn loose. Sometimes she snapped those things and sent me across the living room like I was shot out of a slingshot. I think I was her entertainment center. I really wanted to grow up and get myself a belt.

I had my little brother to teach, you know, the snappin' part, but he was only one and didn't have suspenders yet. Over his diapers he did have plastic britches with elastic around the waist. When the kid learned to crawl, it left the door wide open for snappin'. I know it didn't hurt him because the elastic wasn't very strong, but it sure made a cool noise when you released it.

The best time to do that was right after mama put a clean diaper on him. I put the sneak on him one day when he was really quiet and kinda frozen on his hands and knees right in the middle of his journey across the living room floor. I pulled them plastic britches back to the maximum output to wake him up somewhat. As I was just about to turn loose, I heard a gurglin' noise I had heard once before! I had those britches so tight to his belly and those chubby little legs that nothin' could get out in front. I let them britches snap! A stream of yellow stuff shot straight up his back, under his t-shirt, and up the back of Rugged-Knee's head, leaving a big wad of that stuff in his hair. At this point, I was thinkin' that it was a good thing God put his nose in the front and his rear end in the back. It smelt just about the way it looked, maybe worse. Yup!!

Now I am yelling for my mama to come fix the problem. She came and picked him up like a dirty diaper and the next thing I know he is naked and sittin' in a big bucket on the floor in the kitchen. That aroma sure hung around for a while. (Back then we didn't have air fresheners) Mama was runnin' around openin' windows as fast as she could.

This wasn't the first or last time Rugged-Knee did this. Ever since then, if I was going to scare Rugged-Knee, I always approached just a little off center, even when he was 36.

I did learn one thing that day. If he was quiet and not moving...don't touch him.

Yup!!! Good Times.

***

The first time I remember getting into trouble, I was about six years old, I reckon. My dad got us a swing set and set it up out beside the house. It had two swings, and two bars in between the A frame posts that kept the upright posts from spreading too far apart. It had this other do-dad on there, we called it a seesaw, but might have been a glider. It had two poles coming down from the top with a couple poles horizontal that were about four feet long with seats on both ends, handles up a little higher than the seat, and foot pegs down at the bottom on the vertical poles. Two kids could swing back and forth. I spent many hours on the see saw. It was probably the coolest thing this side of the Mississippi.

Now, Rugged-Knee was a plump little kid when he was one, and he was even a plumper when he was one and a half. This was about the time I took him for a ride on the glider. All he could do was hang on because his short fat legs couldn't reach the foot pegs. I was very careful with him...for a while anyway. He was so roly-poly I had to stop every now and again to straighten him back up on the seat. Heck, with him on there, I couldn't go very high so, every once in a while, I stepped it up a little. I would hear mom yelling, "Be careful!"

"I am," I yelled back. He was doing so well, I decided to step it up a little more. I wanted to go fast enough to feel the wind blowing through my hair, ya know?

Rugged-Knee evidently lost his grip on the handle and launched out into the sweet clover next to the swing that was about three feet high. I could hear him screamin' pretty loud but couldn't see him, as I bailed off of the glider to get over there to make him quiet before mom heard him. That went over like a lead balloon. As I bailed off, my suspender caught on the handlebar and my feet didn't quite touch the ground. I couldn't break loose before the door to the house flew open and mom came out on a dead run. I remember the screamin' from Rugged-Knee and a few choice words from mom. I also remember the swat on the rear end as mom headed out into the clover field to track down the little fat guy. She picked him up and I was still hangin' on the handlebar by my suspender trying to get loose before mom whacked me again on her way back to the house.

Yup!!! Good Times.

***

I can't remember if I've written about my introduction to Jeeps before, but it happened when I was about 6 years old, I reckon.

My mom, little brother and I had gone over to my aunt's house in Absarokee, Montana to visit. I was kinda dinkin' around with nothin' to do. Mom and Aunt Pearl were afraid I would go downtown and catch fish in the fountain behind Aunt Pearl's house. Pretty sure that was the reason Aunt Pearl let me ride her son's old bike, you know, to keep me out of trouble. About a block away there was a road with houses on one side and a field on the other where I could ride the bike.

No traffic at all but there were cars parked in front of the houses.

This bicycle was a boys' bike, a big one too. I had to put my foot on the peddle and hop along beside it until I got up enough speed to hop on and be able to keep my balance. I got pretty good at riding back and forth, back and forth, back and forth on that road and diving in and out between the spaces of the cars where there was enough room to do so. There was a little Willy's Jeep parked in front of one house and there were about two car lengths open in front of it. I would dive in and head right for the Jeep and dive back out real quick, zooming past it. Pretty cool stuff.

After I did this about three times, I heard someone's voice say, "Oh look Gretta, that little boy is really good on that big bicycle." Turns out there were a couple of little old grey-haired ladies sitting on the porch watchin' me ride that big old bike. After another time or two past the Jeep I thought I would show off a little and impress those gals. :) Yup! You know how boys are when they know the girls are watchin'. To achieve the least amount of wind resistance and the maximum speed, I rode in as fast as I could with my head down, my elbows above my head and my rear end up, hangin' on to the handlebars with my hair blowin' straight back. I guess I miscalculated speed and distance and smacked the bumper of that Jeep! I did a somersault, landing on the hood of the Jeep with my rear end up against the windshield. What a crash! It looked like I hadn't attempted to go around it at all. What was I thinkin'?...Kinda like a suicide mission! Those two little old ladies came flyin' off the porch in slow motion worried that I had hurt myself. I hadn't though, and was off the Jeep and almost on the bike again by the time they arrived. (I guess I thought if I was fast enough, those girls would think they had been seein' stuff since I was back on the bike so fast.) They were sweet to think of my well bein' after such a horrific crash. I told them I hadn't felt better after a crash, I hopped on the bike and finished ridin' up the road.

I was so embarrassed all I wanted was some real estate between me and the girls. As I came past the Jeep again, the ladies were back in their chairs on the porch waitin' for the next event to start. I'm pretty sure I was the talk of Birch Street that Saturday. Hopefully my Aunt Pearl didn't hear about my crashin' her son's bike. I headed to Aunt Pearl's house to put that bike away and for Kool-Aid.

Musta' shoved my pride down into my tennis shoes for a spell.

Yup!!! Good Times.

***

I was thinkin' back to the first grade.

The whole year I wondered why the school gave us tiny kids such great big pencils. Remember those pencils big as a horses' legs with no erasers on them and a sheet of paper with only three lines on it? If you were lucky and knew what you were doin', you could get A, B, and C on one piece of paper. By the end of the year, I had myself a regular pencil and a wire-bound notebook.

I learned some stuff with those regular pencils and understood why little, tiny kids shouldn't have the 'cool stuff.' Maybe it was just one little tiny kid.

When I was in my thinkin' mode back then, I chewed on stuff. Yup, my fancy yellow pencil looked like my best friend was a beaver and had teeth marks all over it from one end to the other. Come lunch time, a bologna samich tasted good and shoved the pencil splinters down. My eraser hung on for dear life. Now, this little kid, when he wasn't chewin' on his pencil whilst thinkin', would stick the eraser end in his ear. Yup, one day that eraser disappeared. I was really embarrassed about the whole thing and chose not to say anything to anyone.

Now about that cool wire-bound notebook. While I read in my reader, I took that wire-bound notebook out and ran the wire part back and forth, back and forth, back and forth across my lips, it felt really cool, and my lips went to sleep and were numb. Pretty cool. A few hours later when they dried out, Holy Smoke, I couldn't even smile...chapped lips!!

About halfway through the next year, that little kid who lost his eraser started to get ear aches. Him's mama had to take him to a doctor in Bozeman and have that eraser taken out. That hurt like crazy.

From what I understand, I was always jammin' stuff in my ears and nose...I kinda remember berries up my nose once. I must have kept my mama pretty busy when I was little. She told me I was different from my sister and brothers. Sure love my Mama.

Yup!!! Good Times.

***

When I was about 6 years old, I had a cousin, Judy, who lived at my grandma's ranch. She was the only girl cousin close enough for us to play together. My grandma's ranch was out past our house and we went over there a lot.

I remember once, Judy and I were out playing in the barn when the cows were coming in to be milked. Grandpa and my dad put the cows' heads through a couple of wooden boards standing on end that could slide against their necks so they couldn't pull their heads out. They threw some hay and grain on the other side to keep the cows busy while they milked them. Judy and I were up in the hayloft runnin' around and jumpin' in the hay. Judy jumped over by the wall into a pile of hay and disappeared.

Ya know, from where I was, what I saw was pretty stinkin' cool. I heard her scream and ran over to where she disappeared and looked down through a hole in the hayloft floor. There she was sitting in the hay and grain that the cows were eating. I saw my cousin screamin', her face right up against one of the cow's noses. I'm pretty sure I could see the whites of the cow's eyes and that slimy nose shinin' in what light there was. Judy jumped up and ran back and forth, back and forth until she found a gap she could squeeze through and off she went, slippin' and slidin' in the wet cow dung on the floor behind the cows. She was still screamin'. It sounded like a steam engine whistle that was stuck, stopping only for a second, when she was pickin' herself up off the barn floor. Adrenaline is a splendid thing when you can witness it from afar in action!

Judy's feet didn't touch the ground. She zoomed past the pig pen, past the chicken coop and disappeared onto grandma's porch. Sitting in the hayloft, looking the other direction, I could have told you where she was on her flight to the house by the excitement of the animals.

When I heard grandma yellin, I knew she arrived safely. I climbed out of the hayloft trying to figure out how I was going to explain that it wasn't my fault. By the time I got to the house, grandma had Judy in the yard hosin' her off. Judy told grandma I didn't do anything. Good old Judy! Within an hour, grandma had Judy shiny again. Heck, she looked like a girl again.

Yup!!! Good Times.

***

I had a Hiawatha bicycle when I was little. My brother Rugged-Knee had a little red bike. I'm not sure what kind it was, but it was fast. He'd wrecked it so many times it rattled and clanked. One of the braces was broken on the rear fender and the chain guard was bent so every time the pedal came around, it hit the chain guard and clanked. Helped me know where he was and how fast he was goin'. I bought myself one of those headlights that clamp onto the handlebars and uses flashlight batteries. It was shiny chrome and even had an off/on switch. It was stinkin' cool to ride in the dark.

Rugged-Knee and I were down by Willow Creek Highway near Lane School when it got dark one summer evening. We were going to ride on the gravel road in the dark with my headlight, Rugged-Knee in the left lane and me in the right. Up over the railroad tracks we went, down past the Lane's house and past Hassaker's turn. Grandma's ranch was coming up soon. Grandma had moved into town so there wasn't anyone home. It was spooky and I could tell Rugged-Knee was runnin' out of gas, so we stopped at grandma's old driveway for a rest. We still had a mile and a half to go.

Kinda funny how kids sit and talk and get scared and worked up sometimes. So when I growled like a mountain lion, Rugged-Knee's adrenaline kicked in and he took off! That's also when the batteries went dead on my headlight. I could just barely hear the clank of his chain guard over his yellin'. He'd hunched over the bars and I could see a flash of white from his shorts in the moonlight every time his pedal reached the top. Pretty cool. He was really puttin' real estate between him and grandma's drive.

I rode up close behind him, growled again and the clankin' went faster. As we neared the 90-degree corner, he was still pickin' 'em up and layin' 'em down and his shorts kept flashin', tellin' me exactly where he was. Up over the old highway we went! But then the clankin' stopped and his shorts disappeared for a second, I found him down in the barrow pit bouncin' through the grass but still upright. The clankin' started again and the shorts started flashin' again. One more growl to help him get home faster! Just had to cross our field, down into the ditch, and cross where the fence used to be. There he bailed off his bike before it ever came to a stop at the house and was inside by the time I arrived!

I still don't know how he knew where to go. Even though my batteries went dead, I had back up...Rugged-Knee's shorts.

I had to explain to Mama why he took off the way he did...just scared of the dark I reckon!

Yup!!! Good Times.

***

Due to a previous occurrence at my Aunt Selma's house, I couldn't be left alone there for very long.

My mama reminded me to leave Aunt Selma's bird alone every time we headed to her house. She also wanted to make sure I didn't have my plastic pistol that shoots those darts with suction cups on the end. She thought I might blast the little bird to kingdom come. She searched me before leaving the house and again when we got out of the car.

It seems as though Aunt Selma thought I might hurt her bird or somethin'. I only had him by the beak a little bit one time and it was only for a split second. He didn't come all the way out of that little house, or I would have held the whole bird. He could even still coo-coo when we left. I wasn't allowed within ten feet of the wall the clock was on. Besides, after the "talkin' to" I received, I wouldn't monkey with that little bird again. Oh yeah, mama also tried to get all the extra air out of the seat of my britches for some reason.

One time we stayed till way past dinner, and Aunt Selma seemed to be way too eager to hand me a saltshaker and point me to the rhubarb patch and the apple tree. I really loved my Aunt Selma but that little bird of hers was sure a nuisance.

I guess that is why I still love those old Coo-Coo Clocks.

Yup!!! Good Times.

***

My little brother got scared easily. Picture this...Rugged-Knee was like a spring I could wind up backwards, once the anticipation was built, all I had to do was let go. It's kinda like getting a pep talk in the locker room at half time. You get fired up and you're yellin' and runnin' around inside the locker room anticipating the moment you can get out there and tear up the field. When you finally get the OK to charge out there, the door is locked. Rugged-Knee would explode before ever getting off the bench.

We would hide under something, like a bed or some blankets or in the bow of dad's boat. We would be very, very quiet. Then we'd hear somethin' and whisper, "Did you hear that?" "Yeh." "WHAT WAS THAT?" "Shhhh, quiet!" The noise gets a closer and closer. I can feel Rugged-Knee startin' to shake and his knee is thumpin' against his other leg. By this time Rugged-Knee is wound up tighter than a 30-day clock. His hand is squeezin' my arm so tight the blood flow to my fingers has stopped and my hand has gone numb. I can tell he is gettin' ready to bolt, he can't take it anymore. All it takes now is a little jolt and a loud noise. With my perfect timin', I give him a quick little nudge and yell, "Yikes!" as loud as I can. Rugged-Knee is off like a bullet with a muzzle velocity 3,483 feet per second. This kid is just goin', no idea where and I don't think he cares, just wants to get out of Dodge as soon as possible. To keep the entertainment goin' a little longer, I run few feet behind him and give him some encouragement. The kid has no interest in looking back. His only interest is puttin' some real estate between him and where he was a few seconds ago.

Almost like a fox in the hen house.

Yup!!! Good Times.

* * *

In the summertime when I was growing up, my little kick in the side, Rugged-Knee, and I would head out to have some fun. Mom always told us to stay out of the water. Now I'm guessin' this meant the Jefferson River about a mile away. I can now understand why she wouldn't want us over there. So, I honored her request and Rugged-Knee and I checked out the frog ponds.

The frogs are pretty wise at this pond. The big ones hang out by the cattails at the far end, so we hunt our way down there, catchin' and pocketin' as many frogs as we can. As we sneak along the bank, a big one hops off the bank into the pond and some moss. This frog is big, I'm talkin a handful. Only about 3 feet into the pond from the bank, this big ol' frog's head is pokin' through the moss. To keep from getting wet, we put our toes on the bank and walk our body out over the water and moss on our hands, kinda like you're doin' a push up. So now Rugged-Knee is stretched his full length out over the water and this big ol' frog is now right there in front of him! Being that Rugged-Knee isn't very strong and hasn't done a push up since he could crawl, he is now worried that he might get a little wet. "It's ok. Gosh, just catch the frog and get back to shore." Rugged-Knee isn't the sharpest tool in the shed and can't figure out how to hold himself with one hand and catch the frog with the other...too many movin' parts I reckon. Anyway, he stays stretched out in this push up position for about 30 seconds which must be his limit because his elbows start to shake. Little waves kinda splash out just above his elbows where the water level is and I holler with encouragement, "Grab the frog while you're there." The ripples increase in size and I just know he is gonna scare that frog off. I see how this is going...it's just a matter of time, and the closer to D-Day we get, the volume of the yellin' increases. He is really shakin' now. The ripples have turned into full blown waves going across the pond, and I notice that the frog has now vacated the premises and it looks like Rugged-Knee is alone out there on full vibrate mode. It isn't too long before it happens and he lands face down in the moss and water. Kids Rugged-Knee's age shouldn't know the words he was spoutin' off.

We had all day to get him dry and get the moss out of his pockets, hair, ears, and teeth before headin' home. Mom would never know. It took a few hours, but hey, we didn't have anything else goin' on. Besides, it was fun.

Yup!!! Good Times.

***

Sometimes when you are young, you don't really understand your parents very well. I remember the year I received my famous Hiawatha bicycle for Christmas. This bicycle took me on great adventures, while it learned me some other stuff as well.

I was comin' off the 'Y' about two or three miles from home. Before the interstate came through, the highway ended right there. You either had to go left or right. Calling it the 'T' was out of the question...we already had one of those. Anyway, this road goes downhill for quite a ways and shoots straight over the Jefferson River. A kid can really get going on his Hiawatha! Now, my Hiawatha had been through some rough times but it's the best bike this side of the Jefferson River. I had a pretty good head of steam, standing up, pumping as fast as I could. I was in the process, with one or two more pumps, to be formed to my bike and become air resistant. Then it happened! Yup! I was just about to put my head down to the handlebar with my rear end and my elbows up higher than anything else, when my left pedal decided it didn't want to play anymore and broke off. There are a lot of things that go through a kid's mind when unplanned things happen. My worn-out tennis shoe met the pavement head on. The air hole in the side (to let the smell out) now had my foot stickin' out. The back tire ran over my shoe, but it was still strapped to my foot. And I fell onto the bar of my bike, and I cannot express how that felt...I just knew I would never walk the same again. I was dang near off the bike but managed to stay upright. My handlebars were wigglin' back and forth, back and forth, tryin' to shake me off the bike. I think Hiawatha no longer wanted me aboard and was draggin' me toward the river on the left. I decided to take a hard right down into a draw because I knew my Mama wouldn't want me to get wet. I made it down but only got to see the other side through the spinnin' spokes of my front wheel.

Jeez, I almost hurt myself. There were certain parts of me that hurt pretty bad, and I decided to let the dust clear for about an hour before I tried to get my bike out of the draw. I walked around gatherin' up bike parts and what was left of my tennis shoe (the sole was up around my ankle). I had scrapes all over, but I still had my face, so I was good.

Now that I am older, I can understand why my Mama didn't want me to have a motorcycle.

Yup!!! Good Times.

***

I used to fish a lot when I was young, still do when I can. Most of the time I was by myself. My tackle box consisted of a few hooks, a pocket full of split shot sinkers and a Sir Walter Raleigh tobacco can full of worms and a couple bobbers. Oh yes, and my all-time favorite lure, a red and white daredevil. I can't ever remember going fishing without it or catching anything with my Red and White Dare Devil, but I got a strike once and that made it the best lure west of the Mississippi. Kinda funny what little kids think sometimes.

I had a favorite fishing hole. It was a beaver pond on some backwaters of the Jefferson River. There was an old beaver hut there that had burned. In the evening, I would sit on it and fish for hours. I took my sidekick a few times. I was sure he could catch a fish there and it would give him encouragement to go with me more often. Now, Rugged-Knee didn't have any patience when it came to fishin'. One evening while out there, I would catch a fish every now and then, but Rugged-Knee just caught mosquito bites. I told him he needed to reel in and check his bait. He started to real in and got a snag, which is pretty common for beaver dam fishin'. The kid came unglued, started yelling and, as usual, spoke some choice words little kids shouldn't know at his age. Jumpin' up and down and jerkin' his line tryin' to get it free, he was just about to do the golf thing and launch his pole into the pond when I made him settle down. I don't know if it was a stick, or if he hit himself in the face with his rod when the line snapped, but I had never seen a kid beat himself up before and I don't reckon my laughin' helped his attitude much. I helped him tie on a new hook and some sinkers. When I put the bobber on, I made sure the line didn't touch the bottom of the pond so he wouldn't get a snag. Now he was ready to cast out. He held his pole way back and went to pitch the line out. Who knew it would snag in the willows behind him? I think the kid had it in for himself! He jerked it in the other direction hitting himself in the back of the head. At this point, I was laughin' pretty hard, and if his line wasn't stuck in the willows, he would have likely hit me with that rod. I got that line undone and baited his hook so he could once more try casting. However, the kid was really wound up and threw the line clear across the pond into the trees on the other side. At that point, that little creep pitched the pole down and left for the house, leavin' me all by myself, giggling.

Yup!!! Good Times.

***

So many memories...

When we were at grandpa's, I remember my mom tellin' me a few times, "Don't do that! It makes grandpa madder than a wet hornet!" Heck, I had no idea how mad a wet hornet could get, so to find out... my little buddy Rugged-Knee and I checked it out.

Behind our shed and under the eaves was a hornet's nest. It wasn't big, but it had a bunch of 'em in there. The plan was to pitch a quart jar of water up there and get ready to run. I had Rugged-Knee right there, you know, in case somethin' happened, then he could keep 'em busy while I went and got mom. They musta' heard us sneakin' up on 'em because they met us at the corner of the shed. Rugged-Knee's mouth flew open, "Yayayayay heheheh!!!" He turned and ran into me and I spilled the jar of water. I headed in the opposite direction because the hornets seemed to like him best and I didn't want to break up that friendship. He was on his way to the house, and I was puttin' as much real estate between me and that shed as I could. I stopped about 100 yards out and looked back at the action. Rugged-Knee's legs were movin' pretty fast and even with those big feet he didn't seem to touch the ground. It was almost slow motion, no wonder he couldn't outrun them. There was a little cloud behind him, was it dust or hornets? He managed to only get stung twice by the time he got to the house. I thought he was at full volume while running but I was wrong. Each time he got stung he bellowed like grandma's old milk cow. I came out untouched.

Those hornets were mad, and they didn't even get wet. I think yellow jackets are pretty close to what a hornet is, they just have different houses.

I checked them out today on my computer. Yellow jackets don't seem to like being squirted with a water hose either. So now I know how mad grandpa would get if he was a wet yellow jacket. At least I know after all these years.

Instead of running out in a field, I headed for my oxygen bottle because by the time I got there, I was going to need it.

Yup!!!!!!!! Still Good Times.

***

When I was a little kid my mom used to be afraid to go through my pockets. I remember whenever I was around on wash day, she would make me go through my britches pockets before I could go out and play. I had a pocketknife and a favorite marble that stayed in my britches pocket everywhere I went, but it was the things I picked up on my daily adventures she wasn't thrilled about. I did have some friends I found along the way and would bring home. I remember a cute little snake that she didn't like. He was so stinkin' surprised when she stuck her hand in my pocket and pulled him out. I think all that screamin' scared him. I don't think he liked bein' thrown around the house like that either. He scrambled under the couch and mom never did find him. She refused to sit on the couch. It took a few days, but he finally came out and I had to let him go. I thought that since frogs had legs, they wouldn't bother her. That went over like a screen door on a submarine. So, I decided to hide my little frog friends and put them in my back pocket. This is not a good idea. Moms don't know they are there and sometimes when a kid gets in deep trouble with his mom, he gets a spankin'. Yup!!! My mom had done-in my little toad. Lumpy looked kinda flat, and not breathin' so well. I tried to revive him by pushin' up and down on his belly, but that little croak every time I pushed on him evidently wasn't a sign of life. I made sure he had the best memorial, out behind the shed.

***

When I was around 10 or so, I really didn't get into trouble, mom just didn't care for some of the stuff I did. My dog, Herman, liked to hang out with me a lot. Rugged-Knee used to hang out with us as well. One day we were headed over to "the woods". That is... the big cottonwood trees that ran along the Jefferson River in Montana where we lived out in the country. It was probably 3/4 of a mile over to there, across our field, over a fence, across the irrigation ditch and across another field. Mom always told us not to get wet. Hmm, I think that was her way of saying stay out of the irrigation ditch and that river. Never understood why she didn't want Herman in there, it seemed he was always in need of a bath, both ends smelled the same to me. I guess the good thing was, if it was early enough in the day, if we kinda slipped into the water somewhere, we could dink around the rest of the day until we dried off. A kid just needs water sometimes, kinda brings life into the playground I reckon. Well, it just so happened as I jumped across the ditch to stay dry and out of trouble, I saw something move in the water. It turned out to be one of the biggest suckers I had ever seen. Nope, it wasn't Rugged-Knee, it was a sucker fish! They are only good for kids to catch. So that very moment, I knew we were going to be all day. We chased that sucker all up and down that ditch all day. Rugged-Knee couldn't run very fast in the water because he was still little, so he had to cover the bank. Herman finally pinned that sucker down in some weeds and mud along the edge of the ditch while I scooped him up onto the bank in one motion like a snow shovel. Rugged-Knee was all over him like a blow fly. Since we caught him, we were so proud, we had to show mom! Sometimes little kids just don't think. We still had water runnin' off of us by the time we got home. The good thing was the mud was gone and it was good clean water. It's a good thing we didn't have time out in those days... Rugged-Knee, Herman and I would have spent all our growing up years there.

Yup!!! Good Times.

***

I remember when I was little and couldn't afford 25 cents for a ticket to go to the movies. I'd just walk back and forth, back and forth, back and forth in front of the Ruby Theater in Three Forks and get popcorn drunk from smelling the popcorn.

***

Sometimes kids will do anything to get out of going to school.

We were the first ones on our bus route, so we had to get up early in the morning. Mom used to get us up at 5:30, make breakfast and make our lunches while we were eating breakfast. I can still remember the smell when opening my lunch at school. Mom put our lunch in paper bags with our name on them, sandwiches wrapped in wax paper to keep them fresh. We didn't have much money back then, so it was important for us to bring our lunch bag home with the wax paper so mom could use it again the next day.

We had to catch the bus at 7:00 and Rugged-Knee was always the last one up. I guess you could say he was a sleepy head. One morning while we were eating breakfast, Rugged-Knee fell asleep at the table, sitting straight up in his chair with his elbows on either side of his bowl of oatmeal and his face looking down at his bowl. It amazed me how he could do that. I was eating my oatmeal watchin' him sit there with his eyes closed. I decided it might be kinda cool to see what happened if I kicked the bottom of Rugged-Knee's chair. I crossed my legs and gave the bottom of Rugged-Knee's chair a boot. His elbows flew out to the side and his face went straight down into his groceries. The spoon he had left in the bowl catapulted a full load of oatmeal onto the ceiling, the rest of it spilled down the front of him, covering his shirt and britches. Rugged-Knee's face looked like he'd been hidin' in a wheat field that had already been processed. Mom said, "What the heck happened?" I told her Rugged-Knee fell asleep in his oatmeal. Pretty stinkin' cool stuff. The best thing was, I was the only one that really knew what happened. Rugged-Knee didn't even know. The bus was almost to our house so Rugged-Knee got to stay home that day because there wasn't time for mom to get him in clean clothes. I can still remember the oatmeal dripping from the ceiling while the rest of us kids headed out to the highway.

Yup!!! Good Times.

***

My dad always bought a whole car when he needed only one part off of it. Us kids, but mainly me, would dink around with what was left, get it running, and drive it around in the field. I sold pop bottles and aluminum cans to pay for gas.

One day, I jumped on my bicycle and rode up the highway looking for cans and pop bottles. There was a picnic area at the west end of our field, and I headed there for some bottles. I found a big pop bottle worth a nickel and headed on up the highway on my Hiawatha. I saw a skunk in the ditch and thought to kill it but didn't have a rock to throw. So, I threw my bottle. Killed him dead. He was huge! I grabbed my bottle, and my skunk... to show my dad how big it really was. Bottle in one hand, skunk in the other, I held on to the handle bars the best I could.

About halfway home, that dead skunk came around! Evidently, he had just been knocked out! I had him by the tail, cutting across the field, headed for the house, trying to figure out how I was going to get rid of this wiggling skunk without getting sprayed. I rode my bike as fast as I could, dropped the skunk on the lawn in front of the house and then made a big circle. Things didn't smell so well at this point and, to make matters worse, mom was standing at the kitchen window and just saw what I had done.

Next thing I knew, mom was outside, and I debated riding on down the road for a very long time vs. taking it like a big boy. I stopped and took my *"what for"* from mom. Meantime, the skunk found a hole under the house until dad came out of the house with a gun and shot that skunk way back in the corner under the house.

Guess who had to crawl under there and fetch it? Yup.

And he wasn't smelling so good either.

***

I hope the way my little brother turned out wasn't any of my doing. He did some of the silliest things over the years.

One evening when we were little, I was showing him how cool a magnifying glass was, like using it in the sun to cook ants. He thought that was the best thing since soap on a rope. I went inside for a while and came back out where I had left Rugged-Knee burnin' up ants. He had run out of ants and started on mosquitos. He let them land on him and bite. When they were about half full, he would try to melt their wings so they couldn't fly. He tried and tried. I don't think he ever got the job done, but he sure had a lot of burn marks all over his arm. I thought I'd help him out a little. When a skeeter landed on him and started suckin', I reached over and scotch taped him to Rugged-Knee's arm (Skeeters are pretty tame when they are eating). Rugged-Knee was convinced this was the one that was going to meet his waterloo right there and started to burn him up. I guess scotch tape gets pretty hot when it curls up into a little ball, and it stays warm for quite a while. That was what I understood anyway, kinda sticky and hard to get off. He dropped the magnifying glass and started runnin' around the back of the house yellin' stuff. I think there were some choice words in there. If it wasn't for me, Rugged-Knee wouldn't have gotten any exercise at all.

The next day, I caught Rugged-Knee on his hands and knees lookin' at something on the living room floor. I bet he watched for 10 minutes. When I went to see what was going on, he had a fly scotch taped to the floor. He had swatted it and taped him to the floor. Kinda wonder where he got that idea? It was layin' on its back, its wings all wrinkled. When I asked him what was up, he said, "I'm makin' sure this fly is dead. I swatted one a while ago. He pretended he was dead, his wings were all out of shape, but the little creep flew off after a while." So, I stepped on Rugged-Knee's fly to smash him flat and you would have thought I gave his favorite shirt away. Kinda glad they didn't make duct tape back then. We might have gotten into trouble or somethin'.

Yup!!! Good Times.

***

Georgia and I were going through some old things and found some letters that I wrote to her when I was overseas in the military. Among those letters was a letter to us from Rugged-Knee. To show you how he was, I am going to share the letter exactly the way he wrote it. Rugged-Knee was 17 when he wrote this on July 4, 1971. He was 17 years old. This is the letter exactly how it was written.

Dear Stan, Dorty, and J.C.
Well any way to start out with I might as well say I'm sorry for not writing sooner and about the spelling cause I am. Sorry that is and writing beleave it or not. I would have written sooner but I have really been busy latly. As you know I am working pretty stedy but I've been layed off for the last week and a half. Other wise I've been pretty busy. As you know I recked the Cad and had to get it fixed so our Cad pack has gone to hell. Randys junked his Cad and Carry can't drive any more so really we haven't got a Cad pack any more. But it was fun while it lasted.
Ya know I said I was in busness for my self? Well I still am!! I just haven't sold anything yet but hope to some day. Well really I have sold a record cabnet and a book shelf but I haven't gotten the money for em yet.
You wouldn't beleave what I have been doing the last 4 or 5 days. Working on the truck. I tried to fix the horn cause it wouldn't work all the time so I tore it all apart. Took the sterring wheel off and the turn signals. I stripped the threads on the stearing wheel and took me two days to fix it. I still didn't get the horn fixed but to honk it you reach under the

dash and yank on the wire and when it sticks you beat on the dash and kick the floor until it quits. After I figured all that out I found out the turn signals didn't work so I said the hell with it and went out to Lori's and on the way home the brakes went out and I'm still working on that. When I get the breaks fixed I'll probably find out the tires wont stay on or something weard like that.

Well any way how are ya all coming along? Pretty good I hope. Ya know I really can't think of anything else to say. I guess I'll call it quits for now and watch for your letter to Me. Well bye for now and please take care.

Love Always,
Rod
P.S. write real soon like.
yesterday, OK? OK.
bye.

So, there you have Rugged-Knee everyone. Straight from the Heart and Soul. I THINK EVERYONE NEEDS A Rugged-Knee!!!

YUP!!! GOOD TIMES.

***

From my mom's writing. I'm not sure when she wrote this, back in the 50's or 60's, I think.

For the following reason I am unable to meet your demands for income tax.

I have been held up, held down, sandbagged, walked upon, sat upon, flattened and squeezed by the income tax, super tax, tobacco tax, beer tax, spirits tax, motor tax and every society, organization and club that the inventive mind of man can conceive, to the red cross, double cross and every bloody cross and hospital in the town and country. The government has governed my business until I don't know who the hell owns it. I am suspected, inspected, examined, informed, required and

commanded so that I do not know who I am or where I am, or why I am here at all, all I know is that I am supposed to have an inexhaustible supply of money for every desire of human race, and because I will not borrow, beg or steal money to give away, I am cussed, discussed, boycotted, talked to, talked about, lied about, robbed, held up, rung and damned near ruined. The only reason I am clinging to life at all is to see what the bloody hell will happen next.
Yours faithfully,

The tax payer.

Author, Arleta Carol Thompson Callantine.

***

When I was little, my dad had his own logging business. I remember his boots would be all wet because of the deep snow in the wintertime. One year he logged out of Red Lodge and we moved up in the mountains with him. I can remember it being really cold. If I remember right, it was - 40 degrees Fahrenheit and the snow seemed 10 ft. deep. We lived in a little log cabin with three rooms, two bedrooms, and the kitchen and living room was one. We had a wood burning stove for heat and no power. We used kerosene lanterns for light. Every night when dad came home, he would stick his boots in the oven to dry out. I thought that was pretty cool. When you could smell the leather, he would pull them out and put some concoction on them he called monkey grease, then set them under the stove to dry overnight. Now this stuff really worked to make his boots waterproof. I can't explain how the stuff smelled. The only thing I can think of is a ripe buffalo chip soaked in turpentine. Pretty nasty stuff for little kids to smell all night. It was the only reason we liked to see dad leave for work in the mornings. I loved it up there in the mountains. One night, dad came home and put his boots in the oven. I'm not quite sure what happened, everything was kinda a blur there for a while. Mom was cookin' somethin' on top of the stove and dad was sidetracked reading a book. Us kids were just being kids. When it started to get a little cloudy in the cabin, I saw mom jerk the oven door open and a big ball of smoke belched out like a monster in your closet. It was so smoky in there that you couldn't see anything. Dad jumped up from the table, took a towel, grabbed somethin' from out of the oven and threw it out the door into the snow. Within a second, he came back and did it again. Now this stuff didn't smell very good, and I was hopin' dad just threw our supper out. Things calmed down and after a while... we could see again. Dad had said a few words I had never heard before and mom had somethin' to say about it as well. We did have a pretty good pot of stew for supper though. It tasted great but smelled like burnt leather. Well, actually the whole place smelled like burnt leather for a couple days. The next morning, I couldn't wait to get outside and see what dad threw out. There were a couple of holes in the snow, and I bet I dug two feet before I found the center of last night's attraction. Yup! two shriveled up boots. This is where I decided that the old saying, "Hotter than a burnt boot" came from. My dad started it.

Yup!!! Good Times.

***

I remember a night we spent at my gramma and grampa's house. You know how kids are, well, one little kid anyway. Sometimes curiosity gets the best 'em. My gramma had a bathroom off of her bedroom that I used because the other one was occupied, and I had to do something pretty quick. As I ran through the bedroom, I kinda bumped a little table there by the bathroom door and something fell off. I didn't have time to check it out right then. After I got stuff taken care of, I had to put whatever it was I knocked off back where it had been. As I came out of the bathroom, I looked and didn't see anything, so I dropped to my hands and knees and looked under the bed. Gramma would have my rear end if I didn't put stuff back. I could see it though, a big coffee cup. It must have been full of coffee because the rug was all wet where I lay on my belly to reach the cup. It's kinda dark in there because the curtains were closed. Hey! there was something else there too. I reached under the bed and grabbed it... something wet. When it was close enough to see, I got kinda shaky and tried to turn loose of it but couldn't, so I threw it! It ricocheted off the headboard and into the closet. I could have sworn I heard it whistle! I went to see if my split-second guess was right. Yup, it was! Them there was somebody's teeth. "Man, if I can sneak these out to show Rugged-Knee, he will come unglued," I thought. I could just hear him screamin' when I popped these babies out of my britches pocket. They kinda bulged a lot though. I'd just have to separate them, one in my hip pocket and one in my front pocket. These teeth didn't fit in my britches pocket enough to hide them, and I was sure I'd get caught. Thought maybe I'd just put them back in the cup and bring Rugged-Knee in here. Kinda scary to know that gramma's teeth are in the bedroom and gramma is in the kitchen. As I walked out to the kitchen, I kept lookin' at gramma; looked to me like she had teeth already. She must have extra teeth so if one set is lost, she can still eat.

About supper time, my dad and grampa came in from the barn. It looked like grampa had lost a lot of weight, his face was kinda sucked in. Grampa went in to wash up and when he came out, his face looked normal.

Pretty cool stuff. I reckon I know whose teeth went the rounds with me in the bedroom.

Yup!!! Good Times.

*** *

Rugged-Knee and I used to spin around in circles to make ourselves dizzy. For some reason, this was fun and even funnier when you tried to move right after. One day we put on some good old music and started spinnin'. Rugged-Knee spun half a dozen times and tried to walk over to the chair, but just stood there waitin' for the room to stop movin'. I thought if he spun for a long time, it would be a lot more fun so I helped him get goin' and kept him in one place. I'd shove his shoulders to keep him spinning when he was slowin' down. After a few minutes, I stepped back and started yelling, "Run to the chair!" He started leanin', tryin' to catch his balance. I kept yelling encouragement. His legs were shaky, and he started takin' off. He knocked over the lamp on the end table, ricocheted off the wall and up against the back of the chair. He finally came to rest on the floor almost where he started. He was layin' there tryin' to sit up. That's when...His eyes kinda kept goin' back and forth, back and forth, back and forth. Then his mouth opened really wide, and his lunch made its' exit really fast. The previous commotion goin' on in the livin' room didn't seem to bother mama, but that sound of liquid on a flat surface with a lot of pressure behind it sure did! After talkin' to me about not being a very good influence on my brother, mama convinced me that, since I was in the room at the time of the incident, it was now my sole duty to clean up. Mama also encouraged me to think about what happened and how I could be a better older brother. I did that, just like my mama said. I thought it was maybe best to spin Rugged-Knee outside instead of inside.

Yup!!! Good Times.

***

My sidekick and I used to play cowboys when we were little. We didn't have big boulders to jump off and couldn't get in fist fights with bad guys like Roy Rogers or Gene Autry did.

We would go to the woods and dive over old fallen trees. One time we were running along the edge of a draw that dropped about 10 feet deep. There was a fallen cottonwood tree lying along the edge of the draw. Rugged-Knee and I were getting away from the bad guys. He had a Winchester lever-action rifle, which in reality, was a stick. I had a six shooter and a bowie knife... well kinda, it was a short stick with a knot and a straight stick. But hey, they never misfired and never ran out of shells. So, these guys were chasing and shooting at us. We were running together, protecting each other by shooting over our shoulders from behind trees. We both saw the log at the same time, both thinking it would be super cool to jump over the log, and down into the draw. So, I think I have the timing just right and I told Rugged-Knee, "Lets jump on three! 1, 2, 3... Jump!" Rugged-Knee dove over the log head-first. I didn't do that yet. I wanted to see how Rugged-Knee came out before I submitted my soul to that leap of faith. No sir! This was autumn now, ya know, and there isn't supposed to be water under those leaves. I watched it all unfold from the log. It seemed to happen in slow motion. He landed on his head, instantly turning into a rickety, floppy, somersault - straight downhill, turning into a one-and-a-half jackknife! Almost looked like he was tryin' to tie his shoe in midair. When he hit the bottom of the draw, he had one more bounce left in him. I thought he was going for height on this last trick. I gave him a perfect score of 10. It had scared the heck out of me, but I cracked up laughin', ploppin' down behind the log and bustin' the barrel off my six-shooter. Rugged-Knee was still dishin' out a few choice words by the time I got down there to help him out. We had a pretty good time divin' in the water after that.

We decided to play Army because you are allowed to get wet in the Army.

Yup!!! Good Times.

* * *

My mom thought I picked on my little brother all the time when we were little, but Rugged-Knee wouldn't have had it any other way. He was always stuck to me like Velcro.

One time we were in the bedroom jumpin' on the bed. We always tried to bounce high enough to hit our heads on the light. Rugged-Knee was kinda short, so I lay down on the bed with my feet in the air. Rugged-Knee laid his belly across my feet and I held onto his hands. I could push him in the air higher than he had ever been. "I betcha' I can boost him up to the light." I thought. I rolled back fast on the bed with Rugged-Knee's hand in mine and his belly on my feet, gave a big push up to the light and let go of his hand, not thinking of the outcome until the last second. I launched Rugged-Knee up into the light and everything seemed to pass in slow motion. Rugged-Knee's mouth was wide open, and his eyes bugged out as I watched his terrified face whiten. That was just the trip up. He hit his head on the light and was returning to earth when it dawned on me that something out of my control was fixin' to happen. With cat-like reflexes, I rolled off the bed onto the floor. Rugged-Knee landed on the bed and bounced up against the dresser between our two beds. Just as I stopped screamin', God opened the door to see what was going on. Maybe she didn't see me, so I decided to keep rollin' under the other bed until the smoke cleared. God gave Rugged Knee a talkin' to about jumpin' on the bed and asked him where I was. He said he didn't know, but I had been there a minute ago. God returned to the kitchen for a minute, returned, and flushed me out with a broom.

I got my talkin' to about jumpin' on the bed!

Yup!!! Good Times.

***

Remember those good old days when you learned stuff on your own and remember it like it was yesterday?

I always thought the wind only blew in the spring. After all, that was when the stores had kites for sale. Spring is the best time of the year; everything is brandy new. Brandy new leaves on the trees, brandy new flowers, and brandy new baby aminals. Yup!!! My dad always said, "Spring has sprung, wonder where the grasses is." He was pretty funny.

So, with brandy new everything, all the snow melts out of the ditches along the highways and it's time for me and Rugged-Knee to hunt for pop bottles along the highway so we can get ourselves some spendin' money. Mom went into town about once a week and this time we had the bottles to make it a great trip. I was always pretty wise with my money, but Rugged-Knee, not so much. We had found enough pop bottles that we each got a brandy new quarter for them. Rugged-Knee bought himself a bunch of penny candy and a coke. Back in those days, you could get a bunch of candy and a coke for twenty-five cents. He had a sweet tooth I reckon. On the other hand, I was looking for fun stuff. Yup, spring, when the wind blows and baby aminals are everywhere. I bought myself a kite, a pinwheel on a stick and 5 cents worth of penny candy. When all of Rugged-Knee's candy was gone, I would still have some cool stuff. I couldn't wait to try out my treasures. On the way home I learned what happens to pinwheels at about 65 mph out the back side winda' of your mom's 56 Chevy station wagon. Yup! You wind up with just a stick. Just like a chunk of willow you could have gotten yourself across the lane with your pocketknife, except this one has a little piece of plastic glued to the end of it. Well, I still have my kite and Rugged-Knee made it home with half a bag of candy. I run in the house to put my kite together because the wind is blowin' pretty good. These kites are made of paper and when they are flyin', you can hear the paper rattle. I know because I heard David Phillips's once. I got my string hooked up, ran out past the house and turned my kite loose. It went up about as high as the top of our house and came down with a crash, right into the bushes by the driveway. Who knew that kites needed tails to fly? I didn't see any instruction except that little bit of writin' on the kite. The bush shredded my kite so much I couldn't put it back together again. Wonder if Rugged-Knee still has a little candy he might trade for a pretty cool stick with plastic on the end?

Yup!!! Good Times.

***

Sometimes kids have bad habits. One of mine drove my mom nuts. For some stupid reason this habit seemed to control me and get me into a lot of trouble.

I would pick the elastic out of my socks. It all started outside in the fields, messin' around in the woods. I suppose I was around 7 or 8. I would come home with foxtail seeds, cockleburs, and other weeds stuck in the tops of my sock. You add a little water, about 4 pounds of mud. Let that dry out for a few days and, if you had enough of them, you could probably use them for the foundation of a new house. Mom didn't like to pick that stuff out on wash day. She elected me to do this and sometimes the elastic would pull loose. If you really look at a cocklebur closely, you'll see it is God's Velcro and it works quite well. So, before I put my dirty clothes in the clothes hamper, I had to pick all that stuff out and knock the mud off. I had to do this outside. I'd slam my socks against the clothesline pole out back, then start pickin'. I remember sitting in school and glancing down at a little tiny string hangin' out of the top of my sock. I would pull on that until it broke off. Sometimes it was just a small string and other times a long one. After I pulled one out, another one would pop out of nowhere, so I would pull that one as well. I tried to hide it so no one would catch me doing it.

I always knew which desk was mine when we came back in from recess because of the pile of elastic lyin' on the floor under my desk. After a while, my socks had no elastic in them, and would just flop around on my foot like a hula hoop. I remember running across the field, stopping in mid stride to pull my socks back up. They would always slide down my foot and wad up in the toe of my shoe. That really drove me crazy. I tried to scotch tape them up and it worked until I took a couple steps. I also tried tyin' a string to the top of my sock and runnin it up the outside of my britches and tyin' it to my belt loop. That worked but looked goofy. I didn't need any help lookin' goofy, so I came up with another idea. (I'll tell you what, when I was little, I could fix about anything.) I put my sock on and pulled it up as far as it would go, then folded the top down so it was even with the top of my tennis shoe, poked my shoestring through my sock and tied it. There ya have it, "I fixed it"! The problem was I had picked all the little plastic ends off my shoestrings, so now the hole in my sock for my shoestring was about the size of a 1949 Buick.

I kinda wonder what life would have been like for my mom and I if we would have had duct tape back then.

Yup!!! Good Times.

* * *

Kids do some pretty funny things when they are growing up.

There was a small barn and a corral that circled from one corner of the barn around the front to the other corner. It wasn't real big but had plenty of room for about six horses to run if they were penned up in there. One day Rugged-Knee and I were over stompin' mice and noticed that the horses were corralled and were runnin' round and round inside the corral, so we went over to check it out. The corral was made of lodge poles about 5 feet high. We climbed up onto the top rail and sat to watch them as they ran right past us. We could reach out and touch them when they went by. Pretty stinkin' cool.

Well, when you are double-dog-dared to do somethin', you have to prove the darer wrong, don't you? The dare was for me to jump on the horse's back and grab a handful of mane to stay on. I was pretty sure it would be easy enough. So, I was standing on the top rail hangin' onto the post, getting ready to jump on this white horse. "Watch this... when he comes around, I'll jump." And with nerves of steel, I waited. Rugged-Knee kept sayin', "Jump!" OK, next time I'll jump. After about six of those, I'm still getting those nerves of steel worked up. Now I'm pretty savvy about calculatin' the speed of a horse so I know how much lead I need when I jump on his back. I have all that figured out. (If nothin' else, I'll land a little soon and slide down his neck to his back.) Heck, I've seen Zorro do it hundreds of times! Well, I seemed to have miscalculated his speed or forgotten that horses can stop and go when they want. Heck, they can even turn. Somehow, when I landed, I had planted my butt right between this poor horse's eyes. I think he thought I was a big horse fly or somethin'. So, I slide off his face, not down his neck as planned, and land near a brown horse runnin' beside him. The horse notices the commotion and jumps over me when I hit the ground. Now this is the first time I have seen the belly of a horse while layin' in horse stuff (but not the last). So, I jump up and try to dive between the corral poles to get out of Dodge before they came around again, but I catch my suspenders on a knot. If I hadn't hugged the bottom corral pole, I would have been launched back out into the arena for a second go round. I thought I was goin' to have to leave my britches there to save my life. One thing I didn't want to do was walk home in my shorts and try to explain to mom what Rugged-Knee had done to me. We took the long way home via the pond so I could rinse the horse stuff out of my pants. Rugged-Knee said it was one of the coolest experiences he had ever had the pleasure of viewing.

Moral of the story is to pay attention in school, so you know how to calculate this stuff.

Yup!!! Good Times.

When I was little, it seemed we always got clothes for Christmas and a toy, once in a while. We needed the clothes but seemed to always be able to come up with something to play with. I do remember Rugged-Knee once getting a big battery-operated logging truck with a wire going from the controller to the truck. My older brother got a train set that year also. Funny, I can't remember what I got. I do remember one day tryin' to get Fuzzy to ride on the truck. There were a couple rubber bands that held the logs on, just big enough to go around Fuzzy. He didn't seem to do much except lie around the house all day. Heck, it might be good for him to go for a ride. I did get him to lay on the truck bed, and he even kinda liked it, although it was about two sizes too small. Things were goin' just fine, until I expanded one of the rubber bands to make it over Fuzzy's back feet ...and it slipped out of my fingers! It only snapped once but that dang cat was gone, with the truck bed attached to his side by a couple rubber bands and some scotch tape. Did I tell ya about the scotch tape??? Well, that was what helped Fuzzy stay on the truck bed so well. Fuzzy seemed to think mama's Christmas tree was the best place to get rid of the truck bed after he came out from behind the couch and out from under my bed and the kitchen table. My mama used to have some really cool ornaments on her Christmas tree. She liked to put on lots of tinsel (You know what I'm talkin about?) and those bubble lights. After this little incident, mama told me she was gonna have to chain her Christmas tree in the corner. Well, she kinda yelled it. I didn't even get a chance to try to catch the tree. After the tree hit the floor and the truck bed came off somewhere under the tree, Fuzzy came walking out nonchalantly like nothing important was goin' on, just a few pieces of tinsel hangin' off him. Kinda cool.

I don't remember where Rugged-Knee was during all that, but I do remember trying to tell him that Fuzzy didn't care for the looks of his truck and tried to tear it up.

Well, someone had a lot of clean up to do. It is odd that I don't remember more Christmases. I reckon I have to have excitement to remember them.

Yup!!! Good Times.

***

I used to be Rugged-Knee's savior and guardian angel back in the day. Rugged-Knee was afraid of the dark for some reason, so when it got dark and he had to go to the bathroom, my mama made me walk him to the outhouse about 100 feet behind the house. (Rugged-Knee must have had some bad experience in the dark somewhere at some point in his life).

Once he was in the outhouse and the door was shut, he was good to go, so to speak. I would wait for a few minutes and then scrape a stick across the back of the outhouse real slow and walk around from behind where the door hinges were makin' growlin' noises, kinda low and quiet. I couldn't see him, but I knew he was shakin' because I could hear his teeth chatter and hear him shuffle around trying to be quiet. When I heard him rip a page out of the Sears catalog, I knew I needed to go hide.

He would yell for me, "Stan! Stan!" but the outhouse door stayed shut. I yelled back, "Come on, I'm by the house and I'll meet ya halfway." Dad had mounted one of those umbrella looking lights on the back of the house that lit up the space almost all the way to the outhouse...except a few spots, you know, the ones that had the mountain lions in them. I would hang out by the wood pile about 20 feet from the outhouse. I got pretty good at throwin' my voice, so he thought I was at the house already.

Rugged-Knee never ever waited for me to meet him halfway and walk him back to the house. That toilet door flew open, and he had already taken 5 steps and hadn't made it out of the toilet yet. He hit the trail to the house and the dust was flyin' behind him. He just knew the house was under that light and if he could make it without the mountain lions gettin' him, he was good. After he was well on his way, I ran in behind him growlin', "Grrrrr! Grrrrr!" I got a little closer, "Grrrrr! Grrrrr!" Rugged-Knee threw on the afterburners, but he could hardly run fast. I could tell they were on because I heard him yelling louder. Then I got up right close, "Grrrrr! Grrrrr!" He reached the corner of the house yellin' all the way!

I was just about to turn from mountain lion to angel and save him, when mama stepped out from around the corner. Oops! "Stanley!!! You stop scarin' him. No wonder he won't go outside at night."

I kinda knew I was trouble when my mama caught me in the act of doin' stuff.

Yup!!! Good Times.

***

Rugged-Knee always seemed to be the center of attention when he and I were outside playin'.

One time in the spring it had been rainin' all night and through the morning hours. We were really excited when the rain stopped, and the sun came out so we could get outside. We had one dog that really liked Rugged-Knee for some reason. Wherever Rugged-Knee was, Sneaky Pete was also. I always had to keep a close eye on those two. Sneaky Pete would be out there tryin' to have his way with Rugged-Knee and Rugged-Knee wouldn't make him stop it because he thought Sneaky Pete was just bein' nice. So, every now and again I would have to jump out and yell at Sneaky Pete, "Hey! Cut that out!" Outside in the warm sunshine we were ridin' our bikes through the pud-muddles out in the driveway. We rode around the house, through about six big pud-muddles and back around the house. I was about half a lap ahead of Rugged-Knee. Just as I came around the corner of the house, I got a glimpse of Sneaky Pete running between the parked cars and snagging Rugged-Knee's britches leg. He yanked him and his bike down right in the middle of the biggest pud-muddle. Rugged-Knee was spread eagle on top of his bike with mud and water drippin' off his face. It looked like Sneaky Pete was trying to help Rugged-Knee drown his bike. Sneaky knocked him flat and was all over him like Rugged-Knee was wearin' a pair of pork chop britches.

I came ridin' up as fast as I could to save Rugged-Knee. I thought if I slammed on the brakes and leaned to the side, I could flip enough gravel to discourage Sneaky Pete. Just as I was completing my power slide, with gravel, mud and water flooding Rugged-Knee and Sneaky Pete... wouldn't ya know.... Mama started headin' our way.

Sneaky Pete noticed Mama was comin' too, next I saw, he was in the process of keepin' the deer out of our field... headed towards the woods. It was probably a wise decision on my part to follow Sneaky Pete. So, I headed out back of the house as Mama was draggin' Rugged-Knee out of the pud-muddle. I thought an hour would be sufficient time for Mama to cool down. I remember thinkin' later... 2 hours might have been better. I think Mama holds a grudge.

I have honestly looked to see if Mama has peek-holes drilled, all the way around the house, so she knows exactly when to step out and catch me in the act. How come it's always me she is after? Sneaky Pete started it. Mama doesn't ever seem to get in on the beginning so she would know that I am really helpin' her raise Rugged-Knee right. I can't imagine the trouble he would get into if I wasn't there to guide him in the right direction.

Yup!!! Good Times.

***

When we were in the second and third grade, (and even the second year of the second grade), our teachers would give us important jobs to make us feel good about ourselves and learn to be responsible. They would choose one kid each week for these jobs. So for all three of my second and third grade years, I only had two jobs that I remember. Some kids got the good jobs like the "pencil sharpener monitor". That was the job I wanted because you got to sharpen the other kids' pencils and I was really good at that because I spent a lot of time practicing at the pencil sharpener during tests and stuff. I was so good at it that my mom would have my dad unload logs from his logging truck and have pencils made out of them during the summer, so I'd have pencils through the winter months. Yup!!!! I dreamed of having that "pencil sharpener monitor" job. There's nothin' like getting to sharpen the pencil of a girl that you had a big crush on. I did a lot of daydreaming about girls back then. I dreamed of walkin' beside one that I liked or heck, even holdin' one's hand! But gettin' to grind her brand-new pencil into a two-inch stub while I was going' ga ga over her...best job ever!

Over those years I had crushes on lots of girls... a new one about every two weeks, kinda like the song "Down By The Station," Only bein' about girls. I'm not quite sure what the attraction is, but they have somethin' magnetic that sometimes seems better than a good fishin' rod or even a sweet motorcycle. That must be why my wife is my wife. She didn't care what her fishin' rod was like as long as it worked. Most girls are a lot different than what I thought when I was younger. Gosh, they like outdoor stuff like fishin', huntin', shootin', workin on car's, ridin' motorcycles! Anyway, most of the girls I know now like that stuff.

Oh yeah...sidetracked again. I was never allowed the proud opportunity to be the best pencil sharpener in class. I honestly don't think the teacher knew how good I really could be. I think the kids that had that job went onto college and became accountants and auditors. The teacher did know one thing I was good at because I was chosen to do it all the time... clean the erasers and chalk boards during recess. They let me do it during recess because I lived out of town and rode the bus and wasn't able to stay after school. I think my second grade teacher liked how well I cleaned erasers and chalk boards so much that she wanted me to come back and do it the next year as well. She got the short end of the stick though... I went to the other second grade class and did it for the other teacher.

Yup!!! Good Times

***

Do you remember those good old days in, maybe second grade, and the teacher kinda needed some time to herself during the day so she said, "Ok children, let's all fold our arms on our desk, lay our heads down and close our eyes for about 10 minutes." Well, I was the kid that really fell asleep during that ten minutes and it kinda torqued me off when she woke me up. It put me in a bad mood for a spell. Usually had to stay in and write on the chalkboard while everyone else got to go out for recess. How come she didn't have that sleepy thing after recess? I knew I was her favorite student when she sent my mom a thank you card at the end of the year and asked me to be in her class again next year. My mom said the 'note' was my report card and it wasn't because she liked me that she wanted me back.

I can tell you one thing... my handwriting got pretty good.

***

I was a lot more coordinated than other kids my age when I was in the 3rd grade because I spent a lot of time outside playing and running across fields and barnyards. I got really good at dodgin' cow pies out there. You had to watch out for the light brown ones that were perfectly flat and green in the middle. When you stirred them up, they smelled bad! If you accidentally stepped on the wrong one, you would think you were on ice. A big one could even make you do the splits!

I finally learned how to stay out of trouble. Out by the pond the cows had pushed the mud up along the trail they walked and the following year, the grass grew on these piles of mud. A kid could jump from one to the other and get only a little bit wet... and that green stuff came off somewhat easily. By the time I was 10 or 11, I could dodge pretty well, side-step, catch myself while doing the splits and not even touch the ground... I had really good timing! But to hone my skills, I used my little brother Rugged-Knee and his "dah-dah-ing" skills. I don't know if you know what that is. That is when a little kid sits on a couch, chair or car seat and bangs their back and head against the back of the couch. The couch springs thrust his body forward and then pushing back and banging it again and it just goes on and on. Kinda like pumping a swing... pretty cool stuff. My little brother was always "dah-dah-ing". Rugged-Knee had a special place on the couch that he would do this. He would be "dah-dah-ing", back and forth and back and forth against the couch for hours! You could be anywhere in the house and would know where Rugged-Knee was when he got into this "dah-dah-ing" mood. So, I honed my timing skill using Rugged-Knee's constant "dah-dah-ing". I could run by as fast as I could go, and while on-the-move, I would drop a peanut butter and jelly samich between Rugged-Knee and that couch, and then be out the door and into the field before he knew what happened! Learned not to do this when mom was around though... that's where I honed my runnin' skills. Rugged-Knee dah-dahed for a few years... I think he was 27 when he quit. I guess he got frequent headaches from his head hittin' the wall. He would even bounce on the spring seat on an old Fordson Tractor we had. I got pretty good about slippin' a few bird eggs in the seat when he was in is upward motion, I guess it kinda ruined his day.

Yup!!! Good Times.

***

Rugged-Knee had some pretty light fingers when he was little, only about 8 years old. I remember him messin' around out by the gate one day, so I wandered out there to see what was happenin'. He was munchin' on somethin' and smokin' a cigarette. I think Rugged-Knee was on his way over to the willows where Mr. Sprinkle had his cows. I knew he could get behind the willows and smoke cigarettes and mom couldn't see him. On this day, we had just come home from our cousin's house and he was evidently havin' a nicotine fit right there by the gate and lit up a smoke before he even made it to the willows. I asked him what he was chewin' when I walked up and that little thief had a whole pocket full of milkbones and doggie biscuits he had 'discounted' from our cousin's dog. I guess he had been gnawing on biscuits when he needed a smoke and couldn't snitch one from mom's pack. I thought I could squeal on him, but that didn't seem right either. I had known he smoked but hadn't realized he was hooked on it to the point of gnawing on dog snacks. Heck, it seemed like he had just graduated out of his bouncy chair.

It wasn't but a couple weeks later when my dad finally caught him. "This should be good," I thought. I sure didn't want to be very far away when thiscame to a head. My dad had rolled his own smokes and I know Rugged-Knee was talented enough to do the same. Dad rolled up a couple of smokes for Rugged-Knee that were as big around as a horse's leg... then sat him at the table. I peeked through the kitchen window watchin' this all go down. Dad made Rugged-Knee puff and inhale, puff and inhale, over and over. When he was finished with one, dad fired up the next. Rugged-Knee wasn't lookin' so good from where I was standin'. He started to shake a little and I thought he may be goin' into convulsions, but then puked all over the table. Dad was pretty quick and slid back to get out of the spray. He was prepared though and had towels and a washcloth for him. Evidently, he had experienced the same at one time. While Rugged-Knee was pukin, dad was rollin' him up another smoke. About halfway through that one he puked again. Holy Smoke! I ain't ever seen anything like it. This was the beginning of Rugged-Knee's "No Smokin'" program.

Mom got the short end of the stick, I think... cleaning crunched-up milk bones and dog biscuits off the table, wall and floor. Dad was out three fat smokes and Rugged-Knee was pretty green for a while. Me, I was blessed with a great family memory!

Yup!!! Good Times.

***

I remember one thing that Rugged-Knee and I used to do. We used to kick cans down the road. I know a lot of kids did it but not to the extent that we did. I didn't seem to have much trouble finding things to do and Rugged-Knee counted on me to keep him busy. One day we were walkin' along the highway down in the ditch. In some tall weeds, there was an empty Hamm's beer can someone had thrown out the window of their car. I could tell because only Hamm's had that color. This can was laying in the weeds about 6" off the ground. So, I kicked it. Who knew that there was still stuff in there? Rugged-Knee sure didn't, and I could tell by the choice words he was using that he didn't appreciate the smell of Hamm's beer all over him. Now this little creep wanted to get even, so he ran after the can and tried to kick it back at me. When he kicked it, another batch of beer shot straight back at him. He was so mad he just plopped down in the ditch on his butt. When he came to his senses, he decided he'd throw the can at me. I was good at readin' his mind and raced to kick the can away from him. Now this is the point where he will cut off his legs to get even. I think this is how the game of soccer got started. Every time Rugged-Knee came anywhere near a can, I kicked it away to keep him from dousin' me with leftover beer. Somehow, I missed one beer bottle down by the picnic grounds that wasn't empty and he dumped it on me. Now we are both smelling like beer and afraid to go home because I'm sure mom wouldn't like the smell either. ONLY one thing to do! Yup...go swimmin'! So, we found an irrigation ditch full of water and played in it for a while. Since we needed to dry off, we found a couple more beer cans, empty ones, and continued kicking them down the gravel road towards Lane School. We kicked those cans all the way there, about 3 miles from our house. Now we are dry and can't smell any beer, so home we go. I think mom was watchin' us somehow 'cuz she asked about the beer smell first thing. I asked Rugged-Knee if he could smell any before we headed home and he said no. Do you reckon he was gettin' even, or couldn't smell?

Yup!!! Good Times.

***

We got most of our meat by hunting. I pretty much grew up eating venison. I remember mama wasn't a big fan of venison so she would disguise it in a lot of different ways. She had a ritual performance she went through each evening we were having venison. She would drag out a big old cutting board and she had this special hammer. Now I think the hammer was used years and years ago for opening the armor the Knights used to wear. It had a short handle, but it had two sides. On one side there were raised teeth like a Great White Shark. The other side had a whole bunch of smaller ones. I remember mama hammerin' our steak into hamburger. I think mama also thought that if she cooked venison steak on hot-hot for a little longer than you're supposed to, and changed the shape of it, just maybe it would taste a little better. One time I came into the house when mamma was workin' over some steak for supper. She hammered until the 5-inch steak was about a foot across. Then she floured it, added salt and pepper, threw it in a big cast iron skillet at about 12,000 degrees and slapped a lid on it. I was thinkin' this was going to be the best supper ever with all those big steaks, a bucket of mashed potatoes and gravy and it looked like she was heatin' up some corn.

I made sure I didn't go very far when I went outside. Didn't want to miss out on this supper. About half an hour later I heard words I always liked to hear, "COME AND GET IT". I was in the bathroom in a flash, washed up and at the table waitin'. Mama had covered all the food so it would still be warm when everyone arrived. I was ready to dig in. I got myself a lot of mashed potatoes and gravy and corn and my dad took the lid off of those big ol' steaks. What the HECK??? Those foot-wide steaks I had seen earlier were now little three-inch square chunks of charcoal. I knew mama burned it so she couldn't taste it. I didn't say a word so mama wouldn't feel bad. As I jabbed my fork at one of those great lookin' pieces of steak. it shot to the other end of the platter! I lost my manners and grabbed it with my hand. It's on my plate, but I have to pin it against my pile of potatoes to get my fork into it. Everyone at the table is laughin' and dad asked me if I need him to hold it down while I cut it.

Turns out, it was probably the best steak I ever had!

Yup!!! Good Times.

***

When I was about eleven or twelve my dog, Herman, went everywhere with me and Rugged-Knee. He was an Australian shepherd and had some bad habits. Mama said he was a nasty, stinky little dog but I thought he was the best. He liked to play in the river, the ponds, the creeks, and... oh yeah, the sloughs! To Herman these were the best thing since soap-on-a-rope. I think he liked the smell of the sloughs, which were pretty nasty when stirred up. Herman liked Rugged-Knee the best, kinda liked to rub all over him because Rugged-Knee couldn't run fast enough to get away from him. Herman would knock Rugged-Knee down and wipe that stuff all over him.

We would get home and mama would send Rugged-Knee outside with Herman. Herman loved old dead stuff like skunks and cows. He had the best sniffer this side of the Mississippi and could find a dead cow anywhere. He just liked to wallow in old dead stuff and then wipe it on someone. Whoever could run the fastest was safe from Herman. Herman liked old dried-up cow pies too, and seemed to know when they were just right for wallowin' in, especially those that were just crusted over but still slimy inside. You know, the ones we used to call slip 'n slide.

Herman had a bad habit of draggin' his rear end across the grass because he itched sometimes. He would plop down and start pullin' with his front feet, musta' felt good because he held his nose straight up to the heavens as he went. Herman had another bad habit, as many male dogs do when there aren't any female dogs around for miles. This one got Herman into a lot of trouble. If Herman came along when Rugged-Knee and I headed out across the field, I'd have to keep lookin' back to make sure Rugged-Knee was alright. More than once, Herman would trip Rugged-Knee and have a hold of him before he hit the ground. I always had to carry a big stick and had Rugged-Knee trained to yell out when Herman got in one of his moods. But really, no one was safe from Herman.

One time I was in the house and heard Rugged-Knee out back yelling, "HELP, GET HIM OFF OF ME, HE'S KILLIN' ME!" I went runnin' out the door, around the house and saw Herman had Rugged-Knee pinned. Rugged-Knee was on his knees hangin' onto the clothesline pole with both hands, tryin' to stand up while Herman had him in a bear hug around the waist, havin' his ever lovin' way with him. That dang dog! Could have hurt the little creep.

Yup! Mama didn't really want any of us in the house for very long.

Yup!!! Good Times.

***

I missed out on some stuff when I was little, by livin' in the country and all. My friend lived in town and had a lot of cool stuff, like a sidewalk and even stairs in his house (so he could use a slinky)... heck he even had a fence! I remember playing at his house with some kids who lived close to him and we all played until about 12:00 midnight, sleeping outside in the yard. HIs little sister had a tricycle that we borrowed to do some racin' with. One of the kids had a Hiawatha bicycle that he got for Christmas a couple years earlier. (That was before I broke it.) We were havin' some drag races from the alleyway to the end of his block. I could put my foot on the back of David's sister's trike, push with one foot and lean over the seat, steering with the handlebars. Yup! Kinda like a scooter. David gave me a run for my money when the front wheel of the trike hit the raised part of the sidewalk. I think they are called frost heaves. Well, frost heaves and kids pushin' trikes don't mix well. David was able to ride my bike right over that raised spot, but I was pushin' really hard, and going really fast when the front wheels of the trike stopped all of a sudden! This was the first time I had rolled a trike and believe me; the outcome was worse than I expected. By the time I was finished flippin' over and the trike came back to Three Forks, I had lost the race. I had a skinned-up elbow, a couple scrapes on my knees and a bloody nose to boot. Kinda sad when ya get in a fight with a trike and wind up losin'. I remember dirt and sky, dirt and sky, dirt, trike and sky. I was pretty sure I was going to have to get a job to pay to fix that trike. It had a broken axle, a bent-up fender, and needed a new paint job. David was laughin' so hard! He said I didn't have to fix the trike or get another one... turns out he had pulled that one out of the city dump.

Yup!!! Good Times.

***

My dad was quite the hunter. I figure he must be the best hunter around, except for maybe Davy Crockett...I can't ever remember hearing about dad killin' a bear when he was only three. But, I learned a lot from my pop about huntin'. For instance, "the first shot you have is going to be the best shot you'll get". I can't remember my pop shooting at anything more than once... seemed to be once is all he needed. I wanted to be a good hunter like dad, so I practiced sneakin up on stuff, like rabbits and gophers...and Rugged-Knee. I remember having a BB gun although I'm not sure where I got it. Must have traded somethin' for it. I saved up 10 cents and bought myself a pack of BB's.

A corner of my grandma's field was loaded with gophers. I was goin' to show grandma I could get rid of them for her. Heck, I had 250 BB's to get the job done. I would sit in the field right in the middle of the gopher patch and shoot at them. My prime target was this one gopher that came out of his hole every couple minutes. I lay down flat about 10 feet in front of his hole and waited. Sure enough, he came up, I moved a little, and he went down. Again, he was up and then he was down. This went on for a few minutes and I thought, "I'll be ready so all I have to do is pull the trigger." He pops his head up but I need to see just a little more of him and then I'll let him have a BB with his name on it. *When there are things God wants you to remember, he lets you see it in slow motion.* That gopher was lookin' straight into the barrel of my BB gun when I pulled the trigger. It was the best shot I had ever seen by anyone. I saw that BB come out of the barrel and it collected that gopher square between the eyes! I also saw the gopher blink when it hit him and saw his butt as he went right back down the hole. I think my BB gun had a muscle velocity of about 14 feet per second, but it didn't dawn on me that since he was so close and I could still see the BB, that it wasn't traveling very fast. Heck, I don't think that BB even bent the hair between his eyes or gave him a bloody nose.

I took my gun back home and came back with a fishin' pole, put a loop around the hole and waited. I caught that little twerp and took him home. Yup! Now I have a pet gopher, with a dirty spot between his eyes.

Yup!!! Good Times.

***

I guess sometimes kids see and learn a whole bunch of stuff they are not supposed to see or learn.

One afternoon in my hay days, (I was 11 or 12 years old.) I was walkin' home from town. Most of the time, I cut across fields, runnin' so I could get some dodgeball practice in. You know, dodging cow pies, and jumpin' fences. This particular day I had walked toward the overpass, over the R/R tracks, and jumped between two box cars landing in a pile of really tall grass. I heard a bunch of commotion goin' on and some fella yellin' a bunch of stuff kids weren't supposed to say back in them days. I peeked over the grass to see a Shetland pony runnin' hell bent down the ditch, with a fella hangin' onto a couple ropes and a rope tied to a wagon doodad. The wagon hit a badger hole or an ant pile or something and launched this fella about 10 feet in the air (...okay maybe 4 feet) and started draggin' him through the grass. The pony finally stopped, the fella ran up to him, squared off and threw a left hook. *Holy smokes!* I got down in the grass lower than a snake with no legs. I peeked through the grass with my eyes buggin' out. The pony made a left turn real quick and when that fella's wagon caught up to him, he was all over the place. He tried to keep his feet under him and his mouth never missed a beat. I thought I was at a heavy metal concert for a minute. The fella really wanted to clean this little horse's clock and go to fist-city but I guess he decided the horse had had enough. I think the pony won that little bout. Boy, you should have seen that little wagon after a few more pile drives. Looked to me like it had a broken axle and needed a paint job. I could hear that fella sayin stuff for quite a while along the tracks. Kinda crazy, but also kinda fascinating, ya know what I mean? I think sometimes kids get a charge out of a little excitement.

Yup!!! Good Times.

***

I remember when I was little, around 12 I reckon, my mama would tell me almost every weekend where I was allowed to stray off to. We lived a mile outside of a little town in Montana called Three Forks... a great place to grow up. The town was not quite 1,000 people and they were the best people on the planet. We were very poor, but boy did we have fun. I trekked all over the valley and my mama was afraid of what I might do.

I would walk or ride my bicycle everywhere and there was no limit! Okay well, maybe a little. I was restricted from crossing the river, which ran about a mile from our house. Mama said there were rattlesnakes on the west side and none on the east side. (After thinking on that for about 30 years, I finally decided mama was probably just joshin' me so I would stay closer to home.) I remember I did ask my dad one day if rattlesnakes could swim. He said they could, but they held their tails up out of the water. I figured they did that to keep their tails from rusting. So one day I saw one doing it, and that dang thing swam right towards me. I got a big stick and kept hitting him with it until he swam back across the river where he came from! I guess he didn't get the memo from mama that he wasn't supposed to be on the east side. After that I figure he got my memo. Sometimes ya gotta beat it into them.

My mama could always tell where I had been all day from the cockle burrs and grass seeds in my socks. She also knew if I crossed the river, and which pond I was playing in. I think it was from the moss and mud she found in my clothes. That and the frogs and little snakes in my pockets. I think mama was afraid I'd collect one of those rattling snakes. She made me go through my pockets on Saturday morning wash day before I could go anywhere. I think she was afraid of what she might find in my pocket. (She did find a snake once when I was about 4.) I had the best life and the best mama west of the Mississippi.

Yup!!! Good Times.

***

One time after I had thought my dad had lost a 10 ft. utility trailer he used to have...I found it, out in the backyard, underneath a pile of old boards and stuff. This thing still had air in the tires and I realized I just gotta see what's in the bottom of it!

So I found my little kick in the side Rugged-Knee munching on his samich and convinced him to help me unload that stuff. We unloaded the front of the trailer first, because it was on the ground and Rugged-Knee could reach it better. After unloadin' some heavier stuff from the front, the tongue of the trailer flew up from the weight still in the back. It just so happened Rugged-Knee was standin' close to the tongue with his samich in one hand and a board in the other. When the tongue flew up it caught Rugged-Knee's little mitt hangin' onto his samich and launched that sucker clear over to mom's clothesline. *Hey! Now this is pretty cool.* Well, Herman had been watching, just waiting for Rugged-Knee to set that samich aside for a second. He didn't miss much when it came to food and he got the samich before it hit the ground! (Herman was your best bud as long as you was eatin' somethin'.) It broke Rugged-Knee's little heart that Hermon polished off his samich. He started cryin', the dirt just runnin' down his cheeks. I felt so sorry for him I had to go in and make him another one. Besides, I had plans for that trailer, and I needed Rugged-Knee's help to have some more fun. I found out that you don't want him standing there to make sure you make his samich right. I didn't know there was only one way to make a peanut butter and jelly samich. You do NOT put peanut butter on one slice of bread, then jelly directly onto the peanut butter! No sirree! You put peanut butter on one slice of bread and the jelly on the *other* slice and *then* combine the two. Oh yeah, and when you hand it to him, that stinkin' peanut butter better be on the bottom half, where his thumbs go. I had to make that sumbitch all over again because I handed it to him wrong. *Holy smoke!* No wonder mom gave him lunch money when he was in high school. Well, now it's too stinkin' late to go play on the trailer. We will do that tomorrow I reckon.

Yup!!! Good Times.

***

I stepped out of the house kinda lookin for somethin' to do one Saturday. I saw smoke comin' out of our shed out back and knew that Rugged-Knee had swiped another cigarette out of mom's pack on the table and was in the shed havin' his way with it. (He was only about 8 years old but smoked like a hundred year old chimney.) So, I figured I'd start my day by scarin' him a little.

So, I put the sneak on and once I was at the door, I jumped up into the shed hollerin'. Rugged-Knee started yellin' and rearrangin' stuff in the shed. For an 8-year-old, he sure had a foul mouth, always seemed worse when I'd just appear out of nowhere. When he finished, which didn't take but a few seconds, I started snoopin' in a big box dad had in there. I found a lariat. At least, I'm pretty sure that's what it was.

I got Rugged-Knee to head out into the field and we decided to go across the lane to Mr. Sprinkle's place. He has a calf that isn't quite a cow yet. Mr. Sprinkle's place has some low land that is full of willows and water in the spring. There's a big wooden gate you can drive through if you need to. I think Mr. Sprinkle was trying to keep the calf away from him's mama, Mr. Sprinkle's milk cow. Rugged-Knee and I had just climbed onto the corral pole gate when the calf came runnin' by. "Hey! The next time that calf comes runnin' past, let's catch him with this lariat." I decided to tie the rope around Rugged-Knee so he could help me haul the calf in... and when that calf came runnin' by, I threw the loop *(a perfect throw!)*. That calf headed for the willows lickety-split! He jerked the rope out of my hands and if it wasn't for suspenders... Rugged-Knee would have just gotten his shorts dirty because his britches would still be there beside me. The calf and Rugged-Knee left my presence pretty fast and it took Rugged-Knee's britches an extra second to catch up. That calf was headed for Dodge and puttin' some real estate between us with Rugged-Knee doin' some plowin' and maybe a little fertlizin' along the way!! Rugged-Knee always yells when he's scared, and this was no exception. Once they hit the willows, I still knew exactly where they were from the shakin' willows and all the yellin'. Kinda had a furrow to follow too.

Every time the calf stopped, Rugged-Knee stood up, tried to get the knot loose and his suspenders would snap his britches back up and the dirt would fly. When I popped out through the willows... the calf took off again. Thank the Lord for suspenders.

I finally put the sneak on that calf and was able to jump on him so Rugged-Knee could get the rope off. With all the dirt, water and willows, Rugged-Knee's suspenders were off kilter, and he came out with just a few scrapes, but his britches sure got a workout!

Through all this, the cow was on the other side of the fence just watchin' the whole thing go down, pacin' back and forth.

Yup!!! Good Times.

***

When I was around twelve a friend of mine named Gene (AKA Bean) had this big dog named Rex. Rex was a cat hound. Not sure if you know what that is, but it's a dog used for chasin' mountain lions. Rex was pretty big, retired from that work because apparently he liked to chase deer more than mountain lions. He was an adrenaline junkie, I think. Rex would come out to my house to play with my dog Herman. I could never get any huntin' done with those two around, so I tied Herman up to the clothesline pole and headed for my friend's house with Rex, about a mile walk. Gene had a big bag of Milk Bones for Rex and he let me have some for Herman... gave me a paper bag full. So, I grabbed the bones and headed home so I could get in some gopher huntin'. On the way home, while I was walkin' on the back road with no one around, I was a little hungry and decided I'd give one of those bones a shot. (Have you ever tried one of those??) Those dang things weren't half bad! It was a pretty fair-sized morsel, about the size of my hand. By the time I got home, I had eaten half a dozen or so. Ya know, those things really make ya thirsty. I untied Herman on the way to the garden hose, turned the water on and drank... and drank. I gave Herman one of those bones and he chomped it right down and drank some more. I'm really not sure, but I think that stuff swells up when it gets wet. Kinda makes ya sick if ya eat too many of 'em. Decided not to go gopher huntin' afterall. me-n-Herman just lay in the grass in the shade watchin' the clouds go by.

Yup!!! Good Times.

***

When I was younger, my sidekick Rugged-Knee was a kick in the pants. One day we decided to ride our bicycles into town and go over the viaduct that went over the RR tracks as you come into town. If we could get our bicycles to the top, I figured we could really get up a head of steam going down the other side. I told Rugged-Knee to stay at the top until I got down to the bottom so I could see him zoom past me. The town side of the viaduct had a curve in it, so you start out going East from the top and then north by the time you hit the bottom...unless your name is "Rugged-Knee". So, I rode my bicycle really fast down to the bottom and slammed on the coaster brakes in the gravel at the edge of the highway. I lay a big old skid mark in the gravel about 30 ft. long. *Pretty stinkin' cool!* Now I turn to watch Rugged-Knee. Down he came, leanin' over the handlebars, his butt way above the seat, his elbows stickin' up in the air above his shoulders...he was peddlin' as fast as he could. About 75' before he got to me, something started to go haywire and his foot slipped off of one of the pedals. At this point, I knew this had disaster written all over it. Now, Rugged-Knee was sittin' on the bar and that one foot that slipped off was now above his head. His handlebars were shakin' back and forth so fast he could hardly hang on and it almost shook his shirt off of him! He was headed in my direction fast and I just had enough time to drop my bicycle and get out of the way. Now this kid is frozen in the saddle and at this point he is just along for the ride. As Rugged-Knee went by, his eyes were as big as dinner plates and he was yelling a bunch of words my mom said we should never use. As he crashed into my bicycle, he launched into the air, ass-over-tin-cup into a clover field. As he was in the air, I could still hear those choice words. Once he stopped bouncin, I thought about going over to see how he was doin' but I was laughin' so hard I couldn't see very well, kinda blurry. Overall, he just got banged up a little. I told mom I thought Rugged-Knee needed to go to church.

Yup!!! Good Times.

***

When I was about 12 years old or so, I wasn't afraid of anything! Well, kinda. One day my little brother and I were out playin' around in this big hole. My dad had plowed it out with a caterpillar when he was going to build our house. His plans changed in the spring when the hole filled halfway up with water from the snow runoff in the mountains. I guess our basement was put on hold indefinitely and it became a playground for Rugged-Knee and me. The highway was about 100 yards from our house and the hole was about 100 feet from the house. There was an outhouse about 100 feet out back of the house and about 20 feet from that was *"the Dragon"*. The Dragon was the burning barrel for our garbage. This was like a magnet for Rugged-Knee. He sure liked fire. When mom headed towards the burnin' barrel with the garbage, Rugged-Knee would be like a cougar sneakin' up on a deer. He would peek over the edge of the basement hole until mom had gone back into the house. Then he would sneak around through the sweet clover on his hands and knees because ma would watch for him.

I remember one time she didn't start the fire, she just threw the garbage in. Kinda wrecked Rugged-Knee's day. When it got dark, the little twerp sneaked out there and lit up the garbage. He always had a stick handy to poke at the fire and was stirrin' the pot. He liked to watch the sparks fly up. I figured this was the perfect time to scare the bejesus out of him when he was out prowlin' around at night like this. Over the years, I know he wet a lot of britches when he wasn't expectin' to in times like this. So, I jumped out from behind the outhouse and growled like a lion. But just as I did that, I noticed he was in the process of pitchin' somethin' into the fire. But, he had missed and I got a quick glimpse of it as he picked it up and dropped it directly in the barrel.

"What was that?" I hesitantly asked.

"A shell"

"What kind of shell?"

"A shot gun shell" he said.

Holy moly! That thing had been in the barrel a hot second when I grabbed Rugged-Knee by the arm and charged for open range, tryin' to get as much real estate between us and the Dragon as I could! I knew it was gonna puke! We made it about 75 feet before the Dragon blew. *Holy-mackerel!* It made quite a bit of racket, sparks flew up over the top of the toilet and mom sure came out of the house in a hurry. Rugged-Knee couldn't seem to explain why the Dragon's bottom was blown out and I didn't offer any input. That was one time I was scared for sure.

Yup!!! Good Times.

***

We moved into a motel for the summer when I was about 13. We lived on the second floor, and the stairs went up to a balcony that went all the way across one side of the motel. Kids who've always lived in the country and are used to havin' pets all the time, need some. Rugged-Knee and I bought two little lizards that turn the same color as whatever they are sittin' on. We didn't have anything to put them in, so we just let them run loose in a plant mom had on the table. Mom would plop her purse on the table whenever she came home, and those little lizards would sit on the handle of it. *Pretty cute!* We would sit for long periods of time watching them catch flies. They loved those little fruit flies and there was no shortage of those. Rugged-Knee and I named them. His was Sally, and mine was Sam. We could tell them apart because

Sam was bigger than Sally. One day we couldn't find Sally. We hunted all over, but she was nowhere to be found. After a week or so, we decided Sally must have had enough and left our house for greener pastures.

One day mom went to get groceries and I put in my request for bananas to help draw food supplies in for Sam. When mom came home, she wanted help bringing the groceries upstairs, so I went to help her. I gathered up an arm load and was following mom up the stairs and that is when I saw Sally. *Holy Smoke!* And here we thought she had left us for better adventures. After I set our stuff down and mom started putting things away, I told Rugged-Knee that I saw Sally. He started jumpin up and down and wanted to go catch her. "Where did you see her?" he asked, heading for the door.

I said, "Right here!" I flipped mom's purse on its side and there she was... stuck to the bottom of mom's purse, flat as a piece of paper. Looked like an old dried-up oak leaf with her tail stuck out like a leaf stem. Looks like she was brown when she had met her waterloo. I scraped Sally off into a paper bag with a shoehorn so we could give her a proper burial. We could have just dropped her in an envelope I reckon. Rugged-Knee decided to bury her at sea... he flushed her.

Yup!!! Good Times.

***

I remember tryin' to teach my little brother Rugged-Knee some stuff. I didn't realize at the time what a tough project I had taken on.

One day we were messin' around on a homemade utility trailer dad had out back. You could walk to one end and it would flip the other end up in the air. *Kinda cool!*

We would place an empty soup can on the grounded end, then run and jump onto the higher end to make it fly up in the air, then we would run back and try to catch it before it hit the ground. I was pretty quick and could catch it almost every time. Rugged-Knee... not so much. Hims had a hard time getting started so I would give him a little shove to help get him goin'. I guess he must not have liked me helpin' him out. I could tell because he would walk around in circles lookin' straight at the ground, then say he had to go to the bathroom and head for the house.

While I waited, and waited, *and waited* for him, I came up with new ideas for the soup can toss. So, I went to the house to see what the hold-up was, and there he was, the little creep, sittin' at the table eatin' a bowl of cereal. When he finished, we finally went back out and I showed him that we could lay a log on the ground and put a board across it like a teeter totter, set a soup can on one end and stomp on the other, sending the soup can into the air for us to catch... just like the trailer!

Rugged-Knee couldn't stomp hard enough to make the can fly high in the air. I decided we needed a longer board and a fatter log and headed to the woodpile. I had just seen the board I wanted when I heard Rugged-Knee holler, "I got it!" I looked up to see his adjustments. He'd found a log twice the size of the one that we had. Then he raised a cinder block over his head and down it went on the board. That soup can flew way high. But that short board flew high as well. Unfortunately, Rugged-Knee's cat-like reflexes hadn't come with him that day. The board flew up, smacked Rugged-Knee in the head, his arms flew out, his mouth flew open and he bellowed like grandma's old milk cow! He turned to run for the house, but his workout had just begun. He took two steps, and tripped over the guidewire holdin' the clothesline post straight. He managed to get in about three more steps before my faithful dog Herman came in to make the tackle. Rugged-Knee was tackled flat on his face and that bowl of cereal decided to make its' exit. And he was back up and headed for the house again in a flash.

Well, Herman and I will have to find somethin else to do now.

Yup!!! Good Times.

***

My little brother was kinda hard to get motivated sometimes. I used to "motivate" him quite often, "primin' the pump" so to speak. Sometimes mama shared the motivation part with me, only she used Grandma Addie's recipe for pump primin'. She had an attitude pill that came with a big stick.

Once I took the trainin' wheels off his bike, Rugged-Knee was on his own riding over hill-and-dale. There was no limit, except motivation. That is where I came in. When I wanted him to go for a bike ride with me, I had to motivate him... you know... get him goin'... "kick start" him, I reckon.

Fast forward a few years...

I remember him riding over by the picnic grounds at the other end of our field. He was crankin' on his twist-o-flex throttle and I could hear the roar of that imaginary big old twin engine Harley. As he came barrelin' off the highway onto a two-track road which cut into the field to our house, he hit a badger hole and went head over tin cup. Turned that Harley into a little Honda. Yep, sure sounded different... seemed to change the exhaust system.

After that, it was kinda tough to get him out and goin' again. We would be in the house and I would say, "Let's go ride our Harleys!" He would say, "Naw, not now." So, I would get him excited by playin' go-fast Rock-n-Roll, get him runnin' around and I would holler, "Get on your Harley and ride! Yeah! Yeah! let's go!" I got him all motivated once and we ran for the door and it was locked!... I tried to keep him on cloud nine while I got the door unlocked. We went runnin' out, I jumped on my Harley, and by the time he jumped on his, I was already gone! But, when I looked back, he was headed back to the house. So, I came roarin' back up, slammed on the brakes, leaned sideways and threw the gravel in the driveway with the dust risin' and came to a stop. *So stinkin' cool!* Then I said with the coolest voice west of the Mississippi, "WHATS UP?". He just looked at the ground as he walked, glanced over at me and said, "Mine won't start."

I knew he just didn't want to go on a bike ride.

Yup!!! Good Times.

***

There were once two young boys who lived in a small town and were pretty mischievous. If anything happened, it seemed like they were always involved... somehow. Their mother heard there was a preacher in town who was known to be pretty good talking to kids so she asked him if he would talk to the boys. The preacher was a big man and he said he would but wanted to see the boys separately. So, the mother sent the younger boy in the morning and the older one was to go in the afternoon. When the younger boy sat in the preacher's office, the preacher said, "Where is God?" The little boy's mouth dropped open and said nothing. So, the preacher raised his voice a little, "Where is God?" The little boy still said nothing, so the preacher raised his voice a little louder, "WHERE IS GOD?" The little boy jumped up and ran home and dove into his closet. The older boy came to him and said, "What happened?" The younger boy said, "God is missing, and they think we did it."

***

I can remember building cool stuff with my little brother when I was about twelve or so. But when he got excited, Rugged-Knee's reflexes and thought processes were a little slow.

We lived a mile out of town and had the run of a few miles of land in each direction. We liked to build forts and at times we built booby traps to discourage anyone from strolling too close to our hideout.

We had booby trapped a path through the cottonwood trees and down along a little slough area. We had a tree fort overlooking a little clearing where deer came to feed in the evenings. We called it Fort Somethin'... probably our best fort. It was about 3/4 of a mile from our house. We had planned on going over after lunch one Saturday.

Rugged-Knee was draggin' his feet eatin' lunch so I told him I would meet him over there. I hopped on my bike and rode the deer trail that led to the fort. There were a few places you had to get off the trail and ride through some willows, back down by the slough and up the bank again... on account of those booby traps. By the time I climbed up into the fort, I could hear Rugged-Knee's back fender on his bike rattlin' and his pedal clankin' on his chain guard. I saw a rabbit make a break for some bushes and the birds flyin' up to higher branches. *Him's a comin'!* I peeked over the wall of the fort just in time to see one of our booby traps in action.

In one spot, we had tied back a willow so it would spring across the trail and it caught Rugged-Knee by surprise and put *the fright* into him. I lost sight of him but could still hear the fender rattlin' and clankin', going faster and along the way, the little birds were gettin' out of town. He zoomed past the fort... maybe he had a change of mind? I saw him leanin' over the handlebars with his elbows higher than his head and his rear end up, just pourin' the coal to his crotch rocket... apparently drunk on adrenaline. That was when the second booby trap sprung... a big dried up meadow muffin from some cows that used to inhabit the area. The willow launched that muffin right in front of him.

There must have been just too much going on, I reckon, for the spokes to start working in his memory. Directionally challenged, Rugged-Knee headed down into "no-man's-land"... the slough. As he flew across the slough, he left a trail of leaves and mud to the side, a swath about ten feet wide.

I must have been downwind because the stench of stirred up slough came driftin' through and almost made me puke. By the time my eyes stopped waterin' from the smell... and the laughin', Rugged-Knee had cleared the other side of the slough and was headed for the house... minus his rear fender. His red and white horizontal striped T shirt was customized with a black vertical stripe dead center up the back as he broke through the trees and off into the sunset.

I bet mama had somethin' to say about the smell when he got home.

Yup!!! Good Times.

***

One summer when I was about fourteen, we moved to Pocatello while dad was working at the horse races. We lived in a motel called "The Lazy Dutchman".

I remember it being very hot that summer, and living in town where you couldn't go out into the woods and be yourself was kinda getting to us all.

Rugged-Knee had problems finding things to do... and trying to find a place to smoke so mom wouldn't catch him. He picked a fight with me one afternoon. He was so serious about trying to put the hurt on me that I had to get a hold of him. I wrapped my arms around him, pinning his arms to his body.

He jumped up and down like a pinned rabbit and his mouth flapped, yelling for help. I didn't dare let go until he calmed down. Mom got into the picture and slapped me around some, but at this point she was not as dangerous as Rugged-Knee. So, I just hung on and let her slap me around without trying to get out of the way. But, I turned one time and mom slapped Rugged-Knee instead of me and that only fired Rugged-Knee more that I didn't receive that blow. Mom kept yellin at me to turn him loose.

I said, "I can't, he'll hit me."

She said, "No he won't. I'll make sure of it."

So, I reluctantly turned him loose and he was like a wound-up spring, bouncing around for a minute, but then... he tried to hit me. I blocked his blow and that torqued him off even more. He yelled, and mom yelled, and I told him to go have a cigarette and cool off. I just didn't understand why he was so stinkin' mad!

What was missin'? Maybe he didn't think I loved him anymore because I hadn't played a joke or scared the crap out of him for a while.

Yup!!! It's a lot better livin' in the country than in the city.

Good Times.

***

I was 14 when I did this little deal. I saved up my money and bought a car, a 1956 Pontiac. I named it *"the Pinto"*. My friend Ralphie, Rugged-Knee and I were coming back from Pony one day when I blew a tire going around a corner and rolled my beloved Pinto. Now I had a wrecked car parked out behind the house that needed some care. This thing was definitely out of commission. So, I decided since the motor was good and the tranny was good, I would just build me a hot rod. Yup, a boy and his dream car. The things you can do with "not much" is amazing!

I found another old car out by the river that had been put in on a bend so the bank wouldn't wash out. It was a 1928 sedan with the pooched-out trunk. I didn't take the whole car because it was put there for a purpose and hey, all I wanted was the trunk. So, with a few hacksaw blades and a good pair of gloves I spent two days cutting the trunk off. I drug that thing about a mile to get it back home. My dream was coming true!

The back of Pinto was twisted so I cut it off. I had everything in place except a shorter drive line. Now that was going to cost a bit to fix. Hmmm. So, I cut that sucker in half, right down the middle. *Yup!! I know what I'm doin'.* I slid another pipe in the center and drilled holes in it, applied a couple bolts and tightened them up. *Yup, this is going to work just fine.* I put on a fire wall with the windshield frame from another car found in the river, welded the trunk lid shut and turned the trunk upside down. The lid is now the bottom of my little T. I have no doors, but I'm just going to rod around in the field anyway. Gettin' in and out is a snap. I threw the front seat in, bolted it down and... I've got the Little T I'd always wanted! *Pretty stinkin' cute!* It sounded cool too because I used some more hacksaw blades on the exhaust pipe.

I drove out in the field a little bit but didn't go too fast because I felt a little vibration. Still, I'm excited and ask my sister if she would like a ride. I might even let her take it for a spin! She agreed, so we took off. When I got in the middle of the field, I decided to pour the coal to it a little and spin the tires. Well, when the RPM's got up a little higher, that great driveline that had the little vibration in it, decided to let go! It came up pretty hard under the seat and kinda launched my sister out on the ground. Unfortunately, she didn't think that was one bit funny and she gave me some choice words and advice as she walked back to the house.

I heard her all the way home, and that was 10 acres away.

Still. It was a cool Little T.

Yup!!! Good Times.

Growing Up in Idaho

To all my Facebook friends: I really have a hard time being serious about anything. It's just the way I am, I guess. I really don't look at life itself as a joke, but we must make it fun. After all, we only live once, and we are not sure when our time will end.
Just a thought.

***

I never was one to impress the girls. Cripes, I didn't know how. When Georgia and I started going together, she did things that I just didn't understand. I guess that's what happens when you have never gone anywhere or done anything with a girl before.

Once in a while, I would hold her hand when we walked through the halls at school, or when we walked through stores. But one day she walked up to me, wrapped her arms around me and hugged me. I had never had that done before! And while she was huggin' me, I asked her what she was doin'. That was the first time she called me stupid. She said, "I'm huggin' you, stupid." Oh! Well, heck, I didn't know... I had never had anyone do that to me before. That word --stupid--

seems to have become one of her prize pieces of vocabulary over the last years.

We went out on a date one time to the drive-in theater, and I was there to watch the movie. Heck, I paid a couple bucks a person to see it, but she kept spillin' my popcorn getting her face between my face and the movie screen. Now this is something that had never happened to me either. I had never been kissed and I wasn't going to try to do it on *her* first. I didn't know what I was doin', and I had seen only on TV that a lot of guys get the crap slapped out of them for kissin' some girl. I'm pretty gun shy.

However, if she is going to start it, maybe I can kiss her back and get back to watchin' the movie. So, I kissed her back thinkin' she'd leave me alone. Well, I can't remember what the movie was and I can't even remember watching it. I do remember lookin' around and only people in cars with little kids in them were watching. Everyone else was doin' the same thing we were.

After the movie, we stopped to get a space burger and a coke and continued to drag Yellowstone a few times before I took Georgia home. Then we were doin' the same thing we were doin' at the movie, only in front of her house!

Boy-o-boy, if I had known what a date was, I could have just parked out in front of Georgia's house and saved myself ten bucks.

Now after 43 years of practice, I have this huggin' thing down pat. I'll hug any girl that needs one.

Yup!!! Good Times.

Georgie wanted to know what I did all day today. I told her, "Nothin."

She said, "You did that yesterday."

Yup, I hadn't finished yet!

I was thinkin'. When we started out 48 years ago, we didn't have anything. I realized this mornin' that we still have most of it left. Yikes!!

***

One day we were at my parents' house and all the kids were outside playing. After a while one of them came running into the house with three or four other kids right behind them. The leader was yellin', "Look what we found"! He had a baby bird in his hand. You know the baby birds that are stark naked with a big belly? The ones whose beak hasn't gotten completely hard yet and they had lips? Kinda looks like somethin' you'd find in a bowl of Chinese soup. Anyways the nest had apparently blown out of the tree and my dear wife decides we are going to save this little critter. So, we took it home and she fed it bread that was soaked in milk and it started to grow and look kina like a real bird. It was an English sparrow. We bought a big bird cage and hung it from the ceiling in the living room of our trailer. He got to be quite the little character and was learning to fly. Georgia babied this little friend and cherished it. She would open the cage door and go to the kitchen and call the little bird... she called him Tweety. One day, she called him while I was sitting at the table. That little bird hopped to the door of the cage, jumped and was flying right to her. It was losing altitude, but looked like it was okay and wouldn't hit the floor. Unfortunately, we had a couch that had big brown and grey flowers on it and our great cat Fuzzy was hidden among the flowers. Yup!!! Fuzzy saw the whole thing going down and that stinkin' cat jumped off the couch and had Tweety in his mouth before he hit the floor. I think Georgia's mission was to send Fuzzy to the promised land before his time. This, folks, is why I have been so stinkin' good to my wife over the years. I didn't want to go through what Fuzzy did. Georgia was all over him like a duck on a June bug. She had him by the neck before he hit the floor, chokin' him and yelling, "let go Fuzzy, you $#@* *&$% &%$@ cat."

Fuzzy's eyes were about to pop out and he couldn't let go of the bird with all the chokin' goin on. Georgia had him about 3 feet off the floor shakin' the crap out of him, continuing with those names. I was almost afraid to intervene because of the attitude adjustment she was givin' Fuzzy... afraid I'd get the same treatment. When I saw two of Fuzzy's lives head out the door I decided he needed some help. I had to put one hand over Georgia's mouth so she could hear what I had to tell her. With my other hand I grabbed one of hers because she was still shakin' him like she was tryin' to get rice and sugar out of a bed sheet. I told her to let Fuzzy go because he couldn't let go of the bird while she was chokin' the crap out of him.

When she finally let go, it took Fuzzy a while to get some oxygen movin' again. We had a funeral behind the trailer for Tweety. Didn't see Fuzzy around for a couple days after the funeral. Now ya know why I'm a nice guy.

Yup!!! Sad times sometimes.

***

Ya know, I had so much fun with my little brother all the years we were growing up that I didn't even think about what life was going to be like when we got married and went our own ways.

Who would I tease? How in the world was I going to have fun? My answer showed up in a female package that was 16 years old at the time.

She took things a little more seriously than my little pal Rugged-Knee. This 16-year-old girl decided I needed her around for a long time and then... convinced me to marry her. Yup!!! She seemed to be everywhere I was, so, hey, why not? She was pretty cute, and a lot of fun to be with and she is with me anyway.

So, I married her. This was the best buy of the century. I have learned a lot about women living with this young lady, including how to treat a girl and when to keep my mouth shut. Although, I am still in training for this last one. Other things about women... they think way too deep. They take the simplest thing, turn it into a big problem and don't say what they really mean.

For instance, I want to go hunting but I think I should ask Georgia, you know, out of respect. So, I say, "Is it okay if I go hunting tomorrow?"

"WHAT? GO HUNTING?"

"Yeah, I would like to go hunting in the morning, I'm just going up Inman Canyon."

"OH... I SUPPOSE"

So, I'm wonderin' what this little fit was about. Did she really mean NO, but didn't say it and is pissed because I even *thought* about goin' huntin'? So, I asked her if she wanted to go with me, but maybe I waited too long to ask... I don't know.

I asked in the middle of the day, so now I have a mad wife for the rest of the day. Plus, now she is going to be upset tomorrow if I don't get a deer. I might just as well pack my bags. So now I'm to the point where I'm not sure I want to go because if I come home empty-handed, I might not have a home, and if I do have a home, I'll be livin' with a wild cat for a few days.

I finally reckon, "Oh, I suppose", really means NO, and "Oh, go ahead," really means NO, and "Just try", really means NO, and "It's OK" really means... NO.

If she says yes, now that is questionable as well. *It's the tone.* If she says yes and it's a *snappy* yes, that really means NO. She is setting you up, she is testing you... even if you heard "yes" it's probably a NO. Now, a nice smooth "yes", then hey we're good to go, and you can feel good about it and might even have some fun. OR you can do what I did, buy her a gun and have her come along.

One other thing I know... this is her gun, not yours. You cannot use it, not even for a backup. If you touch that gun, you and she are goin' the rounds.

Nowadays, it's like this:

I say, "I have to work this weekend, so I guess I'm not goin' huntin'.

"That's okay, Tim and I can go. We'll be huntin' down by Oxford." Or "My brother and I are goin' huntin' this weekend since you're on call." Or "Dad and I are goin' huntin' down by Bancroft."

Oh how I love my wife!
Yup!!! Good Times.

* * *

I remember falling in love with my wife. We spent every waking hour we could together. I would pass up sleep, breakfast, lunch, and supper to be with Georgie. My mama said, "You can't live on love alone". Georgie's mama said, "If you love him, feed him". Awww!! I get it. I still love my Georgie and she still feeds me. Now I weigh more than I ever have. Did I miss somethin' in there?

Exercise? No one said anything about that.

* * *

I have spent the last two weekends helping my wife with some woodworking projects. *Holy Smoke!* She is the only person I know that can cut a circle on a table saw.

* * *

I used to drive a 1962 Chevy Corvair when I was in high school. The motor went out on it one day, so I found a used one and my older brother helped me put it in on a weekend. I asked him if he'd tightened up all the motor mount bolts while I hooked up the wiring and gas lines. He said it was all ready to go, so I fired it up and ran it around the block. I drove that car everywhere for about a month.

Deer huntin' season comes and my good friend Ray Dell Bosh and I are going huntin'. This Corvair is our new huntin' rig. My girlfriend, Georgia, said her parents would let her go with us. I invited another friend, Lourie. The four of us piled in the Corvair and headed for the mountains on the other side of Mackay, Idaho about 125 miles away. None of us had ever hunted there but from what we heard; it was supposed to be good huntin'.

We got up on the north end of the valley before daylight and headed across a creek towards a canyon up in the mountains. We found some good places to hunt but didn't see anything.

We headed back early so Georgia's parents wouldn't worry. Coming out of the canyon down into the valley, Ray was driving. At the creek there was a dip on each end of the bridge. When we crossed the bridge to the second dip, the accelerator and clutch pedals went all the way to the floor. (If you didn't know, the engine in those Corvairs was in the back) It felt like popping the car in neutral with the gas pedal still to the floor.

Ray hurried to turn the engine off and stopped the car. We all piled out to see what the heck was up.

The Motor Fell Out!

Yup, right out there on the ground under the car lay the motor to my beloved Corvair, our new huntin' buggy, the car I drove to school, and took Georgia on dates with. Right in front of God and everybody, my car spit the motor out on the ground. Ray said, "Now what do we do?"

It was still bolted up to the transmission, but there were two motor mount bolts that didn't get tightened when Ed and I put the motor in. So, I decided to take a couple bolts out of somewhere else and put them in there. (Note: Always carry some kind of toolbox when goin' huntin'.) But those missing bolts were fine threaded... and the only fine threaded bolts on the whole car.

We walked back up the road to see if by any chance we could see one of those bolts. *Yeah, right!!!*

By some *MIRACLE* we found both bolts lying in the road. We were able to get one log under the motor and another one under it like a cross, boost the engine back up, and bolt it back in. We fired it up and headed for home. *Holy Smoke!* Georgia said it was the most bizarre thing she had ever witnessed.

After being married to me for so many years now, she may have changed her mind about that.

Ya know, when I think about it, I don't know if Ray Dell Bosh and I had ever thought about where we would put a deer if we accidently shot one. If we put it across the back over the trunk, it would cover the louvers that helped cool the engine. Sometimes it's good to not get anything while huntin' out in the mountains.

Yup!!! Good Times.

* * *

Tomorrow is another big anniversary, so to celebrate, Georgie and I decided to go to a movie and have dinner out. We went to see "The Accountant" (good movie by the way). Cost 12 bucks, so we decided to share one large drink and one large popcorn. That was 3 bucks more than our tickets! Georgie put the straw in the drink while I paid for them. The popcorn bag was heaping with popcorn and butter, you know, all the stuff that tastes good, but not good for you. Some of the popcorn fell out of the bag and onto the counter, only three pieces. Being the tight wad I am, I scooped them up and threw them all in my mouth. Two of the kernels were pretty good, the other one tasted fine but was pretty chewy. I decided to take it out of my mouth and pitch it in the closest garbage can. When we got into the hallway where no one would see, I spit it into my hand and dropped it in the garbage as we walked by. Then it hit me...that third kernel of corn was the wrapper Georgie took off the straw and wadded up and left on the counter.

Always somethin' to make our day a little bit better.

***

I hunted a lot when I was younger. One weekend about 25 years ago, my friends and I decided to take the whole weekend and camp up in the mountains in southeast Idaho and hunt mule deer. My deer huntin' rig was a 1970 VW Camper. There were about eight of us if I remember correctly and we camped up in a basin. We set up a pretty nice camp and piles of wood for a big fire. There was about two feet of fresh snow on the ground, so the hunting should be pretty good. There was still some light out, so we decided to scout around and make plans for early Saturday morning. We drove on up into the basin and started walking around to see the layout of the land and where the tracks were. A couple guys went one way, and we went another. When it got dark, we headed back, and the others were already there with a big warm fire. We all had wet boots and pants from walking in the snow, so we lined our camp chairs up around the fire. All our boots were lined up around the fire in front of our chairs, drying.

We sat in our chairs, eating a bowl of chili, BS'ing a little, turning the shoes every now and then, kinda like roastin' a hot dog. Larry got up to get something and when he sat back down in his chair, the legs broke completely off! His butt hit the ground and his feet flew straight out in front of him knocking six pairs of boots in the fire! Everyone jumped up and tried to save their boots from becoming breakfast biscuits with short shoestrings. Laughed all night!

I remember finishing the hunt wearing tennis shoes which, without snow, is the ultimate hunting boot. The hunt turned out successful for a few and meant a new pair of boots for Stan.

Yup!!! Good Times.

***

I was talkin' with this fella the other day. He said he was walkin' through the woods and came across a group of animals, a hawk, a lion and a skunk. They were talkin' about who was the fiercest and meanest.

The hawk said, "I can fly high, swoop down and attack without anyone knowing I'm coming."

The lion said, "Well, I am the king, and no one dare comes close to me."

The skunk said, "Well I am the best and everyone runs away when I come around because of my scent".

Come to find out, they were all wrong. A grizzly bear came in and swooped them up and ate them all.

Yup!!

Hawk, lion, and stinker.

***

Some years ago, I went over to King Hill, Idaho to spend the weekend with my friend Ray Dell Bosh. Anytime Ray and I got together, we just winged it. I decided to wear a halfway decent shirt, (that means it wasn't a T-shirt) and a new pair of Levi's.

On the phone Ray said to meet him over at Lee Roy's about 10 o'clock to move some cows over to the rodeo grounds in Glenn's Ferry. When I arrived, Ray and Lee Roy were out in the field, so I headed out there to help them herd the cows to the truck and the loading chutes. I was tryin' not to step in any meadow muffins with my good boots, so I chased cows while dodging muffins. We jammed those cows in a stock truck. Every time I thought we had it full, Ray said, "One more." It was like packin' 67 buffalo into a pickup truck. We got them all in there and ready for the 30 minute ride to Glenn's Ferry. Those meadow muffin machines (AKA, cows) get pretty excited and their insides don't work so well when they are jammed tight to go for a little ride... the muffins turn to soup.

I met them down at the rodeo grounds to help unload, but tryin' to get the cows out of the truck was a problem. They couldn't turn around since they were packed in so tight. Someone had to encourage them to back out. Mr. Fancy Pants (me, of course) hoped he could do it from the side rails of the truck since the muck was stinky, slick and about 4 inches deep... not good placement for Mr. Fancy Pants.

The cows were slippin' and slidin' and that stuff was flyin' all over. One poor cow had slipped and fallen to the floor, where she stayed until the rest were out and she could get up. I was hangin' on to the side boards of the truck giving encouraging words along with a little boot once in a while. When the top rail kinda slipped out of my grasp, I made a desperate grab for the second rail with my cat-like reflexes and managed to save myself. Danglin' about 2 inches above a portable cesspool of slimy cow dung, it wasn't lookin' good for Mr. Fancy Pants! The best thing to do was straddle one of those heifers long enough to get a better hold on the top side rail. And praise the Lord, he let me out of that momentary situation, as clean as a whistle. Now, there was only one more cow to get out... the one that fell. She got up, but while slipping her way out, her back legs slipped again. And there was Mr. Fancy Pants right there to collect a big wad of that stinky stuff on his shirt!

I found a garden hose pretty quick and did a little laundry. Stuff like this never fails when Ray and I get together.

Yup!!! Good Times.

***

About 20 years ago. I went elk hunting one year with my huntin' buddy, Tim. We took horses. Yup!!! I am really great on a horse and understand them completely.

We were high on top of the mountains and started to ride down a ridge when a blue grouse flew up in front of us and scared the crap out of my horse! By the time I got that horse settled down and tied up to a tree, I had a knot on the back of my head from my rifle barrel beatin' me up. You would think I wouldn't sling my rifle across my back every time I get on a horse. Tim and the blue grouse were just sittin' up there watchin'. Horses should come with shocks, so you don't jar your teeth out!!

After tying up the horse, I proceeded to go back over the terrain and pick up stuff like my lunch, one of my gloves and my pistol. Once Tim finished laughing, we went after the grouse (on foot) who had landed in a tree about 20 feet away. We shot about 6 grouse and headed back to the horses. Funny that the shooting didn't bother the horse.

Tim got on his horse with his three birds. I laid my birds and rifle down so I could get my horse. I decided to slip the reins down through my belt so I would have both hands free to pick up my stuff. Yep, this is not the smartest thing to do folks. I picked up my rifle and nap sack with my left hand, picked up the dead birds with my right hand. When I stood up, the horse saw the dead birds and decided to MOVE!

As he started to take off, I thought, "Boy, I sure was smart tuckin' those reins down my belt so he can't run off." Yeah, right!!! It became apparent that horses can jerk a 160 lb. fella around with no problem what-so-ever. And horses can go backwards faster than you think! I got up off the ground and picked the pinecones out of my britches before I pulled my pants back up. It was a little chilly standin' there in my shorts.

I guess what I thought was a slip knot was something you use to pull a water skier or a jeep out of a mud hole. When Tim finished laughing again, he mentioned that some horses don't like the smell of blood. *Then why in the hell was he tryin' to make me bleed if he doesn't like the smell of blood?*

I don't get along with horses. I don't think they like me. Even if I do understand them completely.

Yup!!! Good Times.

∗∗∗

Gosh! I hate it when you misjudge a dip in the yard and you tip forward a bit too far and by the time your legs have caught up to your body, you are a block away from home.

∗∗∗

About 12 years ago, a friend asked me if I wanted to be his partner in a Bass Fishing Club. Heck yeah!!!! So, I joined the club with him and we hit the rivers and lakes in Idaho on tournaments. We would win a little here and there, but it wasn't about winning. It was about having fun. When you are the non-boater, which was me, because my friend had the bass boat, you don't always get to go with your partner. The way it works: the boaters draw a #, that # tells them their position to leave to get to their fishing hole. The non-boater draws a # and that # tells which boat he is to go in. Now all this takes place about 5:00 in the morning by the river or lake where you will be fishing. The key is to have a fast enough boat to get to the fishing hole before someone else.

We were going to fish the Snake River by Massacre Rock. The rules say the #1 draw leaves and as soon as he gets up on plane, the #2 boat leaves and so on. I drew this young man that had a 17ft Bass boat with a 200 hp Evinrude with a 24 pitch on the prop. Now this sucker doesn't come out of the hole very fast, but when it gets crankin, there is nothing but the prop in the water. We drew #8. I think every boat before us was headed for *our* fishin' hole. So, we had 7 boats ahead of us and we were finally off like a shot, balls to the walls and full-power. We passed the first boat before it got a half mile down river. Mind you, there was no seat belt and no windshield on my side of the boat, but driver had a steering wheel, windshield and controls on his side. At this point, I'm scratchin' for anything to hang onto to help keep my ass in the boat. Smooth water would have been a different story, but we had 7 boats ahead of us out there makin' waves. As we flew over the wake from the first boat, I tried to see what the speedometer read while trying to keep my lunch bag on the floor and in the boat with us. I couldn't see the speedometer with all the bouncing around (Boats don't have shocks ya know). I glanced over to the shore where the freeway isn't too far away to get some kind of idea about the speed of this wet rocket. The speed limit on the freeway is 75 MPH and I'm pretty sure we were passin' these guys. We passed a couple more boats and the water finally smoothed out a little. I sneaked a peek at the speedo again... 77 stinkin' MPH!

We pulled into our fishin' hole behind one boat, so we are 2nd and he says, "Let's get ta fishin'!"

I said, "You go ahead for a little bit. I'll start as soon as I get done shakin' and find my lunch."

Yup!!! Good Times.

***

I used to do a lot of hunting, camping, and fishing with my friend Ray Dell. We did a lot of really cool stuff over all the years.

I remember a little hunting trip we took to a place called Myers Cove which is at the end of the road into the wilderness area. Ray borrowed an older and calmer horse for me. This good old horse had a lot of patience with Stan. (I don't pretend to think that I am a cowboy or nothin anymore, but if I can get my tennis shoe in the stirrup, I'm good to go. Horses are a plain pain in the a$$, but I can see a use for them.)

It was still pitch black out when Ray started moving around, gettin' the horses ready to go. I made breakfast and got lunch ready for later. We climbed aboard and headed out. The mountains were tall and long. We wanted to get several miles up the creek bed to the top of the mountain. When we were up the canyon about a mile Ray stopped, got off his horse and started to fiddle around with his saddle. His words to me were, "Aren't ya gonna tightin' up your saddle?"

"What? I thought you put it on right the first time." I wiggled around a little bit. It felt tight to me, so we headed off again. A little later Ray said, "Ya know, you should tighten your saddle. The horses are winded a little. Let some of that extra air out." "Heck no, I'm good."

About 3 miles from camp, we started up a steep hill, going back and forth, switching one way and doubling back again, working our way up. I had my rifle over my shoulder and my lunch in the saddle bags... in this moment I thought "life was good". And as I made the next switch back, my saddle *kinda* slid to the downhill side. "Hm. I'll complete this turn and see what I can do with this silly saddle," I thought. And as I completed the turn, the little slidey saddle thing became *a big deal*. I slid off the downhill side of the horse with my saddle and saddle bags in tow, leaving me in a horizontal position sittin' straight up on the saddle but the saddle is on the side of the horse... and movin' farther down! I came to a stop and looked up at the underbelly of the horse. Kinda like lookin' for a 'made in China' sticker on the horse's belly.

I'm sure this old horse would tell a different story if he could. Ray didn't keep it inside like the horse.

"Don't ya wish you had tightened your saddle when I did?"

His laughter echoed down the canyon past camp and then some.

I now had the saddle, saddle bags and my rifle under the horse. The trick was to get all that stuff back where it belonged. Ray finally got off his horse and gave me a hand.

He sure had a good time. In fact, he is still having a good time with this one. Some people just can't ever let things go.

Yup!!! Good Times.

***

I am really fortunate to have married a woman that likes the same things I do. We hunted, fished, camped, rode motorcycles, snowmobiles, 4 wheelers, and went snow skiing together. My wife likes to compete in everything.

When we went fishin' in the boat, she wanted to fish by the willows, but I wanted to troll, so there really wasn't any compromising. I took her over by the willows. She thought this was the best spot on the lake because she caught a good-sized Bluegill there once three years ago. I got the boat right where she wanted it and dropped the anchor off each end so we wouldn't move.

Now it just stands to reason that if you don't catch any fish within five or ten minutes, or even get a bite, you're not in the right spot. But my wife will not move what-so-ever. I am ready to go now, we have been there for 30 minutes and haven't even had a bite. I'm tryin' to convince her we need to try another spot, but she is convinced there are big fish right here and she isn't moving. Since we are in the same stinkin' boat, looks like I'm not goin' anywhere.

Now it's way past breakfast and headed towards lunchtime. The only thing that has changed was us puttin' fresh worms on our hooks. Why she will sit in one spot for hours on end without even a bite on her line, is beyond me!

By noon I had eaten all the breakfast muffins and drank all the coffee. The next step was either tryin' to talk her into movin' again or starting on the bologna sandwiches and chips.

And then it finally happened! She was ready to move. *Hot Dam!* I reeled my line in. While I was pulling the anchors, a stupid fish saw her bait and bit. *"What the hell?"*

She pulled in a 2 lb. bass and dropped it in the cooler. *Great. We are not going anywhere now!*

I dropped the anchors back in, threw my stupid line back out and plopped down in the seat. And she did her thing… threw her line out, lay her pole across her lap and continued reading her book. She wouldn't even let me fish on her side of the boat! But hey, we are havin' some fun. I'm pretty sure.

Yup!!! Good Times.

***

You know that tingly little feeling you get when you like someone? That is your common sense leaving your body.

***

It was nice out today, so I decided to take a drive to get some pictures of the fall leaves. Some of my friends did that last weekend and got some really pretty pictures. I saw a lot of deer, turkeys, and a few hawks along the way. Now about them fall pictures... sometime between Monday and Thursday, apparently fall fell.

***

I often look back on some of the things I've learned over the years. I remember one hunting trip with my friend Ray Dell. I just knew we were destined to get ourselves a deer that year.

I was brand new married, maybe a month old at this point and Ray, well, Ray was single. So, we headed south to do some deer huntin' in the early morning before the sun came up. We were drivin' my wife's car, the one she bought from her grandma for $30.00. It was a 1949 Chevrolet 4-door sedan, the ultimate hunting machine because in case we got in trouble in deep snow or somethin, we had tire chains.

As we drove through a small town, we could see wheat fields and then mountains. I looked over and saw some head lights over on the mountain. *"Hey, that's where we need to be".* There was a turn out here and a set of tracks headed across the wheat field. *Hot dam!* We are in business!

About 500 yards out in the field near a pile of rock, the frozen dirt got a little slimy. Now at this point Ray is thinkin' we should head back to the highway and I'm with him on that.

As I started to turn, that 49 Chevy went almost out of sight in the mud. Ray was calm as a cucumber. Me, on the other hand, not so much! During the best hunting time of the day we were shoveling mud and throwing rocks off that pile into the holes.

We drove about two feet and sank again. Now this was really getting to me and I was pretty pissed! Ray just watched and giggled every now and then. We had been there all morning and hadn't gotten very far. As the day got warmer it was harder and harder to get out.

I was really torqued and started yelling and throwing stuff. My wife's poor old 49 Chevy was gettin' a beatin'. I was so stinkin' mad I was kickin' the car and hittin' it with the bumper jack. Ray, he was sittin' on the rock pile watchin'. I heard him continue to giggle every now and then. I finally grabbed that bumper jack and swung it across the back window of the car. The window did not shatter, so I tried again. The jack just bounced off.

And that, my friends, was when I realized that beatin' up an old car wasn't getting us out. And maybe I should think about some anger management. Ray, well... Ray was now howlin' with laughter... like he always did when we were in *a spot*.

I calmed down shortly, and Ray thought it might finally be safe for him to get within an arm's reach of me now. Some guys stopped on the highway and helped push us out.

We didn't get to hunt much that day, but I sure was tired when I got home... kinda like I had a fight with a 49 Chevy... and lost.

I guess some people get out of control.

Yup!!! Good Times.

I washed my motorcycle today. While doing that and drying it off, I bumped my arm here and there and it has a lot of bruises all over it. Most people think they are tattoos, but I know the real deal.

I can kick my own rear and win!!

I received a phone call from a friend yesterday. "There's a car show out at OK Ward Park. You should put your motorcycle in it. Hey, if nothing else, they feed ya."

I had always thought I would do that someday, put my motorcycle in a show. I had just washed it, so I was all over that like a duck on a June bug.

I took it over and they had me park it right up front on the sidewalk because I didn't have anything to put under the kick stand to keep it from sinking into the lawn. I felt pretty good because I knew that way people would see it, not because it was right up front, but because they had to walk around it. One more motorcycle showed up so at the worst I would take second place. Which is only the first loser, I reckon.

During the winter, Ray and I used to drive up Scout Mountain south of Pocatello just to see how far we could get before getting stuck. We just didn't have anything better to do, I reckon. So, once we took my dad's 60 Chevy pickup. It was a two-wheel drive truck with a 6 banger under the hood... a "three on the tree". We'd made it about halfway up the mountain when we rounded a corner where the snow had blown off the bank onto the road. It was about 50 feet in length to drive through this 4-foot drift, so I held that old truck's gas pedal to the floor and hit that drift about 30 MPH. Snow flew from there to Texas, and then... we were stuck. Yup!!! Solid. High-centered solid. Normally no one in their right mind would head up at 9:00 PM during this time of the year. Most people because know they can't get very far with the snow. But for Ray and I, we don't care, we are after the fun! So now we are in the middle of the drift, and the only way out is to dig until the truck touches the ground again. And ya know, we knew before hitting that drift that we might not make it. So, we start digging and digging and after about 3 hours and a lot of choice words, we are free. By this time, it is about midnight. As we head for town, we are traveling at about 45 MPH and suddenly all the lights on the truck go out. Then the engine quits, and now we are cannon balling down Mink Creek Road. Ray is yelling something, but I can't quite hear him because I'm screaming stuff as well. Funny thing is that in the canyon, it sure seems darker at 45 MPH than it does at 5 MPH. We finally get stopped and are still on the road... well kinda, and we have no flashlight, tools or anything. So, we start walking to town. This is not the first time Ray Dell Bosh and I walked towards town because our thinkin' had been off a tad. Over the years, it seems to be too common for us to walk a deserted road somewhere. In fact, that is how we met...walking down a road in the middle of the night. I guess it became a tradition. So, the next day my dad, Ray and I go up to see what the heck is wrong with the truck and it turns out we had hit that drift hard enough to shake the alternator wire to the battery loose and it finally vibrated off the battery. ZAP!!!!! Lights out. Kinda funny how some things happen...but pretty cool that we survived.

Yup!!! Good Times.

* * *

I swear as I get older, I am a lot better at singing songs. My voice has smoothed out and sounds so good I don't have to be in the shower. My wife says I need to change the batteries in my hearing aids.

***

When our son was around 5 years old, we lived in a trailer house in a new trailer court just going in. I had just gotten out of the service and we couldn't afford much so we bought a brand-new trailer house. We decided to get ourselves a dog. I can't even remember where we got this puppy, but he was pretty stinkin' cute and we named him Peanuts. Now Peanuts was anywhere there was some action, but mostly in the house. Peanuts would go anywhere we went if we would let him. We had become real good friends with the people that lived across the street from us and they had a girl a little older Jason, and a boy a little younger. There were a lot kids in the neighborhood to play and have fun, as did the parents. One winter we had quite a bit of snow on the ground and I rigged up a harness for Peanuts and he would pull a sled around. I trained Jason to ride on the sled. Now our Jason and Peanuts were really good friends, but Peanuts would mind a lot better than our Jason did. One night we were over at the neighbors drinkin' coffee and playin' cards and the kids were in the house playin'. It was getting late, so we headed for home. Peanuts pulled Jason to the neighbor's house, so Georgia went on home and I hooked the sled up to Peanuts and sat Jason on it. I started to run to the house, but Peanuts couldn't break the sled loose. Apparently while we were visiting, the sled runners had frozen to the ground a little. I told Georgia to "watch this". I ran back over and broke the sled loose for Peanuts. I ran to the house with Peanuts at my heels all the way. Up the steps and inside I went, with Peanuts right along with me. Jason hung on tight to the sled, but when Peanuts and I went into the house, the sled didn't come along. Jason was up against the trailer and the sled was up against Jason, and Peanuts was still tryin' to get to the livin' room. ...Ya know, I really didn't think that would happen.

I just didn't think Peanuts could pull the sled that stinkin' fast! I received a really good talkin' to by Jason's momma about safety stuff, being smart, and makin' good choices in life. Jason was so bundled up he didn't get hurt, just a little snow up under his hood, up his coat sleeves, in his mittens and packed kina tight in his nose. Ya know, I think I even got a talkin' to about the snow in Jason's shorts. Now if you talk to Georgia, she will claim I haven't learned a thing in the last 43 years.

Yup!!! Good Times.

***

Ya know, when it's really hot out and you are ridin' your motorcycle around town a little, it feels pretty good while you are moving and you really don't want to see a red light because when you stop, it is hotter than a burnt boot. A guy wouldn't mind something a little wet and cool to hit him while he is riding down main street, but pigeon poop isn't my first choice.

***

Georgia Callantine and I are going to go fishin' with some friends tomorrow in Island Park. Should be fun. I decided to put new fishin' line on our poles, you know, the line I bought 5 years ago, but it's new and still in the box. Went to get the line out of the tackle box I had been using out on "Arthritis Beach". The thing was full of sand and flies, so I decided to take everything out and clean it and put everything back in again.

I went out to the shed and rummaged around. Found 6 more tackle boxes, a couple more fishin' nets, a box full of fishin' reels, about 8 more fishin' poles, two worm boxes, worm bedding and a piggy in the shed. It got me curious and I decided to see what else I had stashed away and I started straightening out the stuff in the tackle boxes. You fishermen and women know what I'm talkin about here: a bunch of hooks all wadded up together. Some were still baited with dried up worms from years gone by when you could buy a dozen worms for 50 cents, lures that were made out of copper back in the day, sinkers and hooks still together online and stuff that should be in a fishin' museum. These were from the times when your buddy caught a fish and you had something in your tackle box just like what he was using so you cut your line and dropped the whole thing in your box before he could throw out again.

Overall, I came to the conclusion that some stuff is better off just left the he** alone.

Yup! A shed full of good memories. Good Times.

We were getting ready to go to the store about 6:00 and my wife stepped out the front door on the way to the car saying, "I'm going to have a cigarette before we go."

I said, "Well, I won't hurry then."

She said, "It's ok, we'll get to the car about the same time." What a Wisenheimer!!

***

One summer Ray Dell and I went camping and fishing again back in the mountains. You guessed it... we took horses. Another Stan experience with a horse. Those damn critters shouldn't be allowed anywhere around Stan. The plan this time is to ride the horses up a creek so far that the fishin' is super great because no one has fished it. Ray is on his young and feisty horse and I have the same horse I had when we were on a huntin' trip a year or so before. He remembers me, I'm pretty sure. This horse is so good with green horns. So stinkin' gentle that when I get on, I look for a place to put my dime in!!! Anyway, once we have everything ready and tied on, we head out. About every half mile we get off and fish and are having a great time... so far, our normal Stan and Ray Dell trip hasn't begun yet. We decide to go farther up the creek and come to a place where the creek cuts into a big hill. We see a deer trail going up over it. This place is where the hill had slid off into the creek. From the top of the slide to the creek is about 75 feet. We are riding up around this on the deer trail, which is about 10 feet above the slide. Just as we get to the highest point, Ray scares some birds up and spooks his horse. His horse spooks mine. Ray's horse turns around really fast on the trail, but my horse is in the way. My horse rears up on his hind legs and this is when I turn into a piece of Velcro. Now don't quote me on this, but I can't remember my horse putting his front feet back on the ground until he was headed in the opposite direction. I stopped to watch the rest of the show Ray's horse is puttin on. I have no idea how Ray got out of that without gettin' hurt. His horse bailed over the bank *Holy Smoke!!* Right over that bank down to the creek! About 30 feet from the creek, Ray decides to get off. When he bailed off, his horse fell and rolled the rest of the way and dove into the willows at the bottom. Ray's gear is now scattered from hell to breakfast and he's not sure if his horse is OK. From where I'm sittin, *that was pretty stinkin' cool!* Ray walks through the willows after his horse who is waiting on the other side. I think the only thing that was left on that horse was the bridle and his shoes. It was pretty scary, but at the same time funny... maybe not for Ray. I owe Ray a few laughs anyway. Ray still stops by once in a while.

Good friends. Yup!!! Good Times.

***

Since everyone has cell phones now, we don't have a bunch of printed phone numbers in phone books anymore. Our phone book is so thin, I swatted a fly a while ago and all I did was break one of his legs and ruffle a wing. Yikes!!!

***

I really don't know how, but I still seem to get in trouble. Especially with my good buddy... yup!!!! Ray Dell Bosh. One time we went coyote huntin' over by Bliss, Idaho, which is near where Ray Dell lived. My wife was out of town for work this particular weekend, so I called and told her I was going over to Ray Dell's to hunt some coyotes. Her little Blazer gets a lot better gas mileage than my pick-up, so you bet... I'll take that. It's about 150 miles to Bliss and we are going to do a lot of driving out in the desert as well. I just bought a new rifle and I'm excited for Ray to shoot it. It is a 17 cal. and a pretty cool little gun. So, we head out huntin' and callin' coyotes and we are not doin' all that great. I pulled into a place where the gravel road cut through a little hill and pulled over about halfway down in the ditch. The car is out of sight from any coyotes on the other side of the hill. We sneak around the hill, callin' for about 30 minutes. There is nothing out there. When we get back to the car, I said, "Hey let's go ahead and shoot this new gun I bought." So, I get into the back of the car and since it's half in the ditch, it's leanin' towards the passenger's side. I hand Ray the gun and run across the road to the bank on the other side to level a little place to shoot into for a back stop. I set a plastic shell box up and go back to the car. Now Ray isn't a very tall guy, and he is leaning across the hood of Georgia's car and I'm at the back watching. He shoots and asks, "Did I hit it?"

I said, "I didn't see any dirt fly. Hang on, let me go see."

I went across the road and didn't see any sign that he even hit the hill. As I walk back to the car I said, "Heck Ray," and I'm kinda giggling, "I don't even think ya hit the hill." Ray looks through the scope again and says, "OH CRAP, LOOK." On the hood, about 1 foot in front of the windshield, where Georgia is going to sit the next time she drives her car is a dimple. Ray shot my wife's car! *"I'm in trouble!!"* Yup, that stinkin' bullet ricocheted off the hood of her car at about 2400 feet per second and sailed over that hill out into the desert. Being that my wife doesn't know I am out huntin' with her car, I think this 2400 feet per second might be the speed I'm going to need when I tell her what happened. At least I have 150 miles to think about how I'm going to go about telling her... and still have a home. The one good thing I have at this point is that RAY DID IT. I made sure that Ray Dell's house had an extra bedroom just in case this didn't go well, but I decided to just tell her the truth. What can she do? Kick me out, slap me around for a while, throw all my stuff out in the yard and tell me to go stay with Ray? Nah, she did none of that, she just said, *"does the little shit need his butt kicked?"* That's when I told her he told us to get it fixed and he'd pay for it. But when we found out how much the repair shop wanted to fix it, she said she couldn't make him pay for it. I have the best wife west of the Mississippi. She even lets me drive her car once in a while, the one with the dimple still in the hood.

Yup!!! Good Times.

**

It amazes me how far the tiniest smidgen of mustard will go when you try to remove it from your lips, and cheek, and chin, and shirt and pants and shoestring. It's like removing Velcro with a knit mitten. Once you have it, you can't get rid of it.

**

There is a time in life when you think your kids have grown up and you are stinkin' proud of them. Then out of nowhere they let you down.

This happened to me when I was brandy new freshly married, with a brandy new fresh child. I was in the Navy back then, so I reckon I was about 20 or 21. I had just finished Steelworker A-school for the U.S. Navy Seabees, and we were moving from Oxnard, California to Pocatello, Idaho. I know my mom and dad were proud of me taking responsibility, starting a family and serving our country. They had never been to California and decided they would come out to visit a couple weeks early and help us move back to Pocatello. We had a great time while they visited and as we started home, we stopped in Northern California to get somethin' to eat. This is where things got out of control a little... where I found out that my mom still had the ability to slap the crap out of me.

When I was younger, around 10 or so, one of my favorite things to do was to tear off one end of the paper straw cover, stand the straw on end and collapse the paper cover down to the other end like an accordion. It would fold up like a flex hose and only be about a half inch long. Then I would shove this up my nose. When someone was looking, I'd pull on the end stickin' out of my nose and the paper cover would unravel like you're pullin' a vacuum cleaner hose out of your nose. Kinda gave the person watchin' a little buzz, kinda like shovin' a blow fly up your nose. *Pretty cool!* Grossed out a lot of people.

So, ...back to our trip. My mom is sittin' in the back seat of our car and I decide to shove this straw cover up my nose and turn around so mom could see me pull it out of my nose. Just as I turned around, mom was about to take a bite out of her samich and had it up to her mouth. That's when I unleashed the ol "pull the straw wrapper out of your nose trick." Apparently my mom still has her catlike reflexes, and her expert marksmanship. With the speed of lightnin' and without missin' a beat, Mom proceeds to slap the crap out of me with her right hand while she's takin' a bite out of her samich with her left hand.

My mom is really good at doing two things at once. I've had her in training all my life. I still think she was proud of me, though, for the family and my service time anyway. I had one of the best Moms a person could ask for.

Yup!!! Good Times.

***

Rugged-Knee and I didn't have as many adventures together once we moved to Idaho. Getting married and having kids changes life a bit. Here is one of the memories I have from working together at the Volkswagen shop owned by my father-in-law.

My little brother, AKA Rugged-Knee, wasn't the sharpest tool in the shed. He had done some pretty silly things in his life to earn that honor.

I think one of the goofiest things he had ever done was test car batteries with a piece of wire. At the volkswagon shop,he worked out of the back garage door and I worked at the front. It was a nice summer Saturday. It was hot so we had all the overhead doors in the shop opened. He had a VW bus in the back door that didn't get power to the engine or anywhere else. I told him to put the battery charger on it for a while and check out some other things while the battery was charging. After about 30 minutes I can hear him back there yelling and saying a few choice words, so I dropped what I was doin' and headed back there. The poor guy was standing behind the bus where his twist-o-flex watch band was glowing somewhat and still on his wrist.

"Cool!!! What's up?" I asked. He said, *"Get this damn thing off me!"*. So, I grabbed a pair of pliers off the workbench and got a good hold on that twist-o-flex watch which now has all the twist lengths welded together and is now the same size as his wrist...solid like one piece of metal. This thing is hotter than a firecracker and for some reason when I grabbed it, it fell apart and landed on the floor. I did notice there was no gold in that watch and the plastic face cover was melted flat. *It was pretty cool!* Now he had a burn mark all the way around his wrist that looked exactly like his watch. You could see every little detail burnt into his skin. I couldn't find the made in Japan stamp or the Timex stamp, but he sure had a great brand on his wrist. So, here's the story... Apparently, the poor guy unhooked the battery charger and instead of looking on the dial to see if it was charged, he took a piece of bailing wire to strike it from the positive post to the negative post to see if it sparked. *Holy Moly!!!* The wire stuck to the battery and then stuck to his watch band and he couldn't free it until the wire burnt in half which didn't take very long. It's a good thing it was a thin wire, or we would have had a BBQ Rugged-Knee through and through. Boy, he was hot to trot there for a minute. Sure, is funny to hear the things that come out of people's mouths when they get excited. His poor wrist swelled

up and he had to hold ice on it for the rest of the day. But hey, I have not seen him check a battery with wire again.

YUP!!! GOOD TIMES.

***

Well, it finally happened. I waited all day yesterday, all last night and this morning it came. It is a beautiful day. No reason, it's just a beautiful fall day. Have a great day everyone. Just because you can.

***

When my son Jason was a kid, I felt he and I had nothing in common... not one stinkin' thing. Georgia and I tried to get him away from the TV screen long enough to do something like fishin' or huntin'... I even signed so he could buy his own hunting rifle with the money he earned from his paper route. I took him out, taught him how to shoot it, sighted the rifle with him and everything. Unlike me, he did not like to get up early, so I fought him every hunting season morning to get up, get him in the truck, and finally head up into the mountains. Typically, after we would head out hunting on foot, this little twerp would eventually find a way to sneak back to the truck, eat his lunch and mine then take a nap. When we arrive back at the truck, we would ask him if he's seen anything. "Nope, didn't see anything." Holy Smoke! Ya have to open your eyes and leave the truck!

But one year, we went huntin' and we made him walk with us up on the hill so I could see the truck a ways off and could catch him if he snuck back there. So, Georgia goes one way after we get to the top and I go another and our son was to go in the middle. We all split up and Jason heads right back to the truck! Georgia gets where she wants and shoots herself a deer. She cleans it and has it ready to go. I am way off to the other side and I shoot one, get it tagged and taken care of, then I head back to the truck which is 2 miles away. As I am walking on a little two track road, I hear some 4 wheelers coming. It's two old men hunting, and they stop and say, "Do you have a boy up here huntin'?"

I said, "Yes and my wife too."

The one old feller said, "Well, don't know about the wife, but you need to get over the mountain and find that boy. Else, we'll have a freeway to get home on if you don't! He shot a deer and didn't know what to do. We have been riding on all these roads up here, and ran into that boy on every one of them. He has been all over these mountains lookin' for you!"

So, I head out, getting halfway down the back side of the mountain and run across Jason headed my way. He sure did! The kid shot a deer about 75 yards from the truck when he was sneakin' back to eat my lunch and take a nap. As he had never previously been with me when I shot one, he didn't know what to do, and was pretty excited. So, we cleaned it and together pulled it over to the truck. Makes me proud and still to this day...laughin'!

Yup!!! Good Times.

***

Sooo, yesterday, one of the grand kids wanted to go to skate at Ross Park. I said I would take him out there. He was all excited and when we went to get in the PU truck, he called out, "SHOTGUN." ...It was only him and me. Holy smoke!

***

I have decided to share a memory about our daughter, since she is one that I haven't talked about yet. I knew from the get-go that this little girl was going to be a whiz at everything when she was a little older. I'll describe her a little. My hunting partner's wife told me that very thing when we first met over at a friend's house. As I was standing there talking, our daughter was hanging onto my leg, climbing between my legs and then over here and over there. Janet said Nique was "like a fart in a hot skillet". And it's still that way today. Long ago, as we had just moved out of our trailer house and bought the house we are still living in, there was a little old lady that lived next door and her name was Mrs. Cramer. She was about 80 years old or so, and in the evenings, she would stand out in her yard and water her lawn with the garden hose and a sprayer. She has a little fence between our yard and her yard. It is a short pole fence with just two poles high, and about one foot apart, so it is a short fence. Now Nique, our precious little child, is only about 5 years old at this point and she is a cute little stinker, you know the kind... almost 3 feet tall, her front teeth missin' except one that is halfway in. It came in a little crooked, so she has this snaggle tooth and she has freckles up on her cheeks and over her nose. She has really pretty blue eyes and long hair that looked like she brushed it with a rake... no two hairs going in the same direction. She has a dress on with pockets in it and the dress is trimmed in white lace. Her shoes have little buckles on them. She has been playing out back of the house in the dirt, so she isn't very clean, but by golly, she is cute. Do you see her? You know the kind.

I am standing in the yard over by Mrs. Cramer's, visiting with her while she is watering her lawn, when Nique comes runnin' across the yard and grabs a hold of my pocket. She kinda swings around a little, stands up, takes one step beside of me, looks Mrs. Cramer right square in the face and says, "Is that your fence?" Mrs. Cramer giggles a little as she leans down and says, "Yes it sure is my fence sweetheart." Nique says, "Ok!! You stay on your side of your fence and we'll stay on ours." Nique ran back out back to continue playing and left me standing there holding the ball. Mrs. Cramer and I cracked up and she said to me, "OH!! She is a little firecracker, isn't she?" What could I say? "Yes, she sure is." I will never forget that. It was so stinkin' funny comin' from a cute kid. Loved it.

Yup!!! Good Times.

***

We are babysitting our daughter's three little Chihuahuas. One of them (Kody) was already on vibrate when he got here and for the life of me, I forgot where the on and off switch is.

***

Our daughter is a salesperson, I think. She has been selling stuff ever since she could walk. Her favorite customer was our neighbor Mrs. Cramer. I think Mrs. Cramer thought Nique was so stinkin' cute that she would buy anything from her. When Nique was about five years old, she accidently sold something to someone (Mrs. Cramer?). I can't remember what it was, but Nique evidently thought it was neat and sold it. That started something! She would sit at the table and draw pictures and color them. She made these beautiful pictures, usually of a little stick person with a great big head and the sunup in the corner. You know, like one of those bobble head dolls that sits on the dashboard of your car. So, she makes up about a dozen of these different pictures to sell. Now these are original pictures... not prints mind you. I'm not sure how much she sold them for, but they were really good to stick on your refrigerator. She came home one day with a little fist full of coins. This is how it all started I think. Our son, when he was in junior high, played in the band. Yup, he had those dreaded band fundraiser candy bars to sell. He came home with a couple boxes of them and was all fired up to sell them. To help the kid out, Georgia and I bought one. Well, he ate one and Nique had one. That gave him enough change so that if someone gave him a five spot, he could give them change. How cool is that? So, he heads out the door with his boxes of candy bars and comes home about an hour later. Steps in the door and I said, "So how many did ya sell?"

"I just sold one," he said, "and I ate it on the way home." He took his candy bars upstairs to his room and I never heard anything about it for about two weeks when he asked if I would buy another one because he had one more week to sell them. Holy cow! He ate half of one box and brought another box home when he asked me. So now the kid has one week to sell two and a half boxes of candy bars. I was in the living room givin' Jason what for, tryin' to convince him to get his butt out there and sell those candy bars, when little Nik comes wanderin' through. She is probably in about the third or fourth grade at this point. She stops at the hallway door, leans against the doorway with her right foot on top of her left foot, her hands folded in front of her and says, "What's up?"

So I said, "I'm tryin to get your brother to go sell those candy bars."

She said, "Where are they, I'll sell them." He gave her the candy bars, about 40 of them and she took off. In about 2 hours she sold them all. So, I'm thinkin' this girl could sell a tractor to the Amish.

Yup!!! Good Times.

***

Sometimes little things just tickle me a lot. I can remember when I learned to ride a bike. It took me a whole day of trial and error on my cousin's bike. She was a bigger girl and had a big bike, but it was nice that it didn't have that attitude adjustment bar in the middle like the boy's bike did. I can also remember when our son Jason learned to ride a bike. He had a little bike with trainin' wheels on it. He learned to ride out along the side of our trailer house in a trailer court. We lived on a corner lot with a street running alongside the trailer and a street that went down a little incline about 4 trailers down and into a cul-de-sac.

Since there wasn't much traffic through the court, there were always kids on bicycles on the streets. I have no idea where the bike Jason learned to ride on came from, but I do remember about once a week I'd sneak those trainin' wheels up just a little higher. I can remember hearing those trainin' wheels hit the black top once in a while and they would rattle. About every 10 feet one would hit the black top on one side, then the other side. One day I hardly heard them at all, so I decided to take them off altogether. Now that I have them off, I can hear Jason's doing OK.

Now when it's Nique's turn to learn to ride. I decided not to use trainin' wheels. I'll just take this little chic and hang onto the back of her bike seat. She learned to ride pretty quick. I decided to turn her loose down the cul-de-sac. It seemed like a good idea at the time. She was able to keep her balance. I was so excited I forgot I didn't show her how to stop... or steer. But hey, common sense tells ya to turn if somethin' is in the way, right? I am still not sure when common sense enters our lives though...I thought it was natural, born right in there with learnin' to ride a bike.

But, I'm standing at the top of the cul-de-sac watchin' this unfold and it's not lookin' good for Nique. There is one car down there on the side of the street, and for some reason, Nik thinks that as long as she is pedaling the bike won't tip over. She is leaning down over her handlebars pedaling just as fast as she can with her hair blowing in the wind. She was still pedaling when the front tire on her bike collected the rear bumper on that old Pontiac. The car didn't move one inch, but miss Nik flew up onto the trunk and slid back down on top of the bike. By the time dad got there, the cryin' was almost finished. We gathered ourselves up and walked that mean old bike back to the house to try again some other day.

Yup!!! Good Times.

***

I don't know why my wife and I waited so long to learn how to snow ski. Georgia took a class at ISU, just for kicks I think, as she was going for her degree. While my teachers for skiing were my 16-year-old daughter, Nique, and her girlfriends... in particular, Corri and Lisa. Now these two girls were into everything and just pretty good kids. They really liked pickin on dad as well. I let them talk me into going skiing up at Pebble Creek on a night ski trip. I think I wasn't thinkin' clearly that day. Pebble Creek is a really steep slope, but the girls assured me I would be on the "bunny hill". I rented a pair of skis and boots and when I looked down the ski hill, I told Nik I wasn't sure I was ready to go down that hill. So she, Corri and Lisa turned me around, pointed me to the parkin' lot and gave me a little shove down the service road to the parkin' lot. Here's three teenage girls yelling and skiing right along with me. I did not fall and I wobbled only a little, so the girls are convinced I am ready for the "bunny hill". Apparently, Pebble Creek "bunny hill" is an intermediate run anywhere else. So, I look down that hill and I still don't think I'm ready. But hey, the girls want to ski somewhere other than the parkin' lot. We get up there and they tell me to point my skis downhill and go. "Turn sideways to stop Dad... or just sit down."

"Yup, you girls go ahead. I'll ski right across here kinda slow then turn and come back. I'll meet you at the bottom."

The girls ski away down the hill out of sight. I ski across the slope then halfway back, and didn't fall once! That's when I hear the girls laughing and yelling. I look up on the ski lift and there they are, yelling stuff like, "YOU GO DAD, YOU ARE 20 FEET FROM WHERE WE LEFT YOU 30 MINUTES AGO." The girls continue up and ski the hill a half dozen more times by the time I get to the bottom. When I get to the chair lift, they are not to be seen. A young man helps me onto the lift, because this thing doesn't stop or slow down, you need to be ready to be swept off your feet. Just as I settled in, I slowly read a sign that says, HOLD YOUR SKI TIPS UP PAST THIS POINT. Sometimes I wish I would have spent more time reading when I was growing up. Maybe I could have read that a little faster and avoided what was to become the worriedest ride of my life..."SNAP!"...I am now on my way up the ski lift with one ski on and the girl in the chair behind me who now has my other ski.

Now I imagine what it will look like for me to get off the ski chair with only one ski on. I am worried sick about getting off this thing without getting run over by her. I'm in my own personal state of shock thinkin' about this when I hear "THERE HE IS! HEY DAD...WHERE IS YOUR OTHER SKI??" Now I didn't really want everyone on the mountain to know I'm a dork, but the girls aren't proud...they seem to want everyone to know! They are getting a good laugh out of this. I'm pretty sure I hear Nique say, "We've got to see this." I watched them snap their skis off and run like a bear was chasing them up the hill to a spot to watch dad try to get off of this thing. Yup!!! It was kinda like a gunny sack race. I just put my ski down and ran really fast with one leg. Once the action was over, they skied down to the bottom and came up the lift to meet me. It sure was fun, we did a lot of skiing after that.

Yup!!! Good Times.

When I was a little older in life and married with teenage kids, we spent a lot of time on our boat out on American Falls reservoir. One year I found a set of water skis at a yard sale and decided it might be fun. The kids had no problem what-so-ever learning, but they had been snow skiing. So I was the one at a disadvantage. Georgia tried waterskiing once and decided from there on that she would be the designated boat driver. I had finally got the hang of it and thought it was pretty cool. I always had to have two skis, kinda like trainin' wheels to keep me from tippin' over. I got so good, I decided to try some stuff and have some fun. I turned across the wake really fast and caught some air, but I seemed to be top heavy. Oops! I finally got the hang of it by watchin' the kids and asking questions. I'm not sure they were tellin' me the right stuff. I think they were getting even with me for tryin' to raise them right.

One beautiful Saturday afternoon, we invited some friends and relatives out to have a beach party, ski, BBQ and have some fun. We had everything set up on the beach. I was out skiing with Georgie drivin' the boat when everyone showed up. I motioned to Georgie to swing by the beach and I'd let go of the rope and ski in. I don't know why guys have to try stuff when someone is watchin'. Georgie went by once, but I decided I was going to need more speed to make it to the beach. So as she swung around again, everyone was standing on the beach watching and ready. I had swung out like a crack-the-whip kinda thing to get all the speed I could muster...I'm pretty sure I hit 147 mph... and I didn't remember that speed bump being there the first time around. I hit that little bump kinda wrong and my skis went above my head. Unfortunately, it wasn't my skis that connected to the water first. I kinda skipped like a flat rock for a while and, from what I understand, my swim shorts weren't where they were supposed to be. I saw the boat swing around with Georgie at the helm laughin' so hard she couldn't pull the throttle back to slow down. I glanced over at the beach where everyone was doubled over laughin' as well. I knew I had to get my swim shorts back up before I got close to the beach (Good thing one of the skis had kept them on). Sometimes you have to laugh, even when it hurts. Everyone said it was the funniest thing they'd seen in a while. Lots of fun.

Yup!!! Good Times.

***

I remember when Georgia and I were just getting into snowmobiling compliments of (once again) our daughter, and her husband. After a few little trips with them, we thought we would buy our own snow machines. We looked around for some good used snowmobiles and found one that Georgia liked. It was a Polaris 500 Indy RMK, a pretty quick little sled and just like our daughter's. We were eventually going to buy two snow mobiles but had only bought the one so far. We went ahead and bought two helmets... brand stinkin' new ones.

One weekend we went on a day trip in the mountains with our daughter, her husband, and his dad. I borrowed a little 340 from our son-in-law's dad and I am all set. When we get ready to leave the trailer (ya know... we used to live in one), Georgia and I got our new helmets on, but notice there is a clear film piece of plastic over the helmet lens so it didn't get scratched when shipped. So we take that off and head out. It's still kinda foggy out 'cause it's still pretty early in the morning. We are up riding the trails in the mountains and having fun and then head back to the trailer for something to eat. It's still pretty foggy about 1:00 in the afternoon, and sometimes Georgia's desire to beat her daughter at stuff gets the best of her. There is a straight trail, which is really a road that is about 2 miles long and our daughter and her husband are racing each other down this road. Georgia takes off after them riding in the ditch and doing about 60 MPH. Me?... I'm putzing behind because I have the little 340 sled that can't keep up. Pretty soon, Georgia disappears... and a big cloud of snow flies up where Georgia was supposed to be. The snow machine comes flying out of the snow cloud but Georgia... isn't on it. Our son-in-law stops fast and jumps off his sled. By the time I get there, he is digging Georgia out of the snowbank. She is laughing so hard. Turns out, there was a creek there and she flew over the creek and into about 5 ft of snow. There's snow all packed around her face in the helmet. Holy Smoke! She never touched the ground for 30 ft.!! She was OK and we all had a great laugh. So we get back to the trailer to eat something and I notice Georgia's helmet had a crack on the lens, so I get a close look at it. Here is another piece of plastic over the other side of the lens. Looks like they put one on each side from the factory, so there really wasn't any fog... in fact, it had been clear as a bell all day! Just Georgia and Stan were foggy. We had never bought a new helmet before. Yup!!! Good times.

***

So I let our oldest granddaughter use my PU to move out of her apartment 3 weeks ago. She sent me a message Sunday to let me know that she would be returning my truck. Yay! Now I can pull the boat or the trailer whenever I want to. She had left her little car here while she was using the truck and I noticed the headlight covers were all sun bleached, so I cleaned and polished them so the light would shine through. I'm not sure what that thing was that she left here, some little Maserati or somethin'.

Yesterday morning I drove it to the post office to mail some stuff but when I went to remove the key from the ignition switch, I couldn't get it out. ...Well, I'd only be a second, so I'll worry about it when I get home! Afterwards, I went over to the gas station to fill the car up with gas and once home, parked on the lawn so I could wash off the tree seeds and kinda make it look better. When I was finished, I started on checking out that ignition switch. That key would NOT come out of that switch! I tried everything!! Put the car in neutral, push in on the clutch, set the emergency brake, wiggle the steering wheel... I shook, pushed, pulled, and wiggled every damn thing in the car that I could reach and that damn key was still in that ignition! I slammed the door, went in the house and got on Facebook! I sent a message to my daughter asking how to get that key out. She said there was some sort of little button right there by the key slot that you had to push and turn the key at the same time. So, I said, "You stay right here while I go try" Ooooohh! That little do-dad!!!! You have to push it and turn the key towards 'lock'. OH MY HELL!!!!! What were these auto makers thinkin' of? Were they afraid that stinkin' key was goin' to jump out the winda' at 60 MPH? I tell you what... by the time I got that key out of there, I was on 4 liters of oxygen and runnin' a sweat. You would think I was tryin' to get a pill bottle opened! Well, I was finally able to park the little car back on the street, get into the house to tell my daughter it was a done deal without worrying about someone stealin' the car because I couldn't get the key out. Holy smokes!

***

Our grandson is having a sleepover at grandma's house tonight. Not "grandpa's", but "grandma's". He is in the living room watching a movie, and I'm dinkin' around on the computer in the other room. He starts yelling... "GRANDMA!!!"
(And 30 seconds later...)
"GRANDMA!!!"

Well, I don't hear "Grandpa", so I'm not listening.

It goes on and on... every 30 seconds... "GRANDMA!!!"

Well, grandma is outside and can't hear him, but by golly grandpa can and grandpa has had enough! So, I go into the living room to see what the problem is and Matthew is sitting in a recliner with a plastic fork in his hand. So, I said "What seems to be the major malfunction buddy?" He says, "I can't put this in the sink." "Well for heaven's sake why not?" I asked. He said, "Puddy Tat wouldn't let me in the kitchen." We have a big old alley cat that we let come in the house once in a while and clean up the cat food that our fussy little cat won't eat, and he doesn't like little kids. When Matthew went to put the fork in the sink Puddy Tat was polishing Xochi's dish, growled and scared Matthew off. But by golly, it's so stinkin' important to get that silly fork in the sink right now. Holy Smoke!!!

The Midnight Ride of Paul Revere.

One of our grandkids was staying with us for a couple days. I decided to take him for a little motorcycle ride. Holy Smoke what a trip that was! I thought we would ride on the freeway to the town of Inkom, and then back to town on the old road... a little over 30 miles. Before we got on the freeway there was construction and a long line of single lane traffic. We were hangin' out at the entrance ramp ready to jump in, and when I saw our chance, I stepped on it to keep up with the traffic. Oh my gosh!...I realized that this kid had never ridden on a bike! He is 18 years old, about 6'0, and weighs in at about 87 lbs. When I shifted from 1st and grabbed 2nd, he hit me in the back of the head with his helmet. What the heck!! This kid is like a wet noodle back there, floppin' around like those goofy things you see standing next to a business with the fan blowing, makin' them fly around.

We went 55 MPH until we got out of construction. Then the speed limit went to 80... the speed I had planned on. The faster I went, the more he flopped around. I felt him all over the back of the bike. In my rearview mirrors on both sides all I saw was his elbows. I couldn't tell if he was on the bike or stretched straight out behind, holding onto the sissy bar. I checked my mirrors again after going around a couple of semi-trucks and it looked like he had his left hand on his head and his right hand down the back of his pants. I glanced at the foot platforms to make sure he still had his shoes and socks on. We finally got to Inkom and I pulled over to see if he was OK. He told me his back itched, I think. So, we headed back on the old highway riding about 45 mph and he was still wigglin' around back there. I slowed some and turned far enough to yell out, "Are You OK?" I heard a bunch of mumbo jumbo that reminded me of a bumble bee in a soup can and thought maybe he swallered a bee. I guessed he was OK, he didn't jump off.

When we got home, I had to tell him that when we are going around a corner and I am leaning, that he really needs to lean with me, not to go the other way. :)

We'll try again in a few days. Fun times!!!

***

Went to a new place to eat last night with Nique, her friend and Georgia. Before we even had a place to sit, I had to go to the restroom. So, I did and when we got a booth, it was facing the restrooms. There were some ladies sitting at the bar and drinking and havin' a good time. One had to go to the restroom and went in the one I just came out of a few minutes ago. How cool is that she had so much to drink she went in the men's. LOL. Nope, she didn't, our daughter went in the same one. Haha... a community toilet, how about that?

Then our daughter's friend went, and I finally had to ask, "Did you turn left or right?". He said, "Left. The right is the girls'." Oops! I did think it was odd that there were no urinals in there. I also thought it was odd that all the toilet seats were down. No wonder our friends don't want to go out with us. I really have to start proofreading a little better.

Yikes!!!!!!!!!!

Gotta love life.

***

When you have a big bowl of ice cream and tip the chocolate syrup bottle up and it takes you a long time and you get too much chocolate syrup on your ice cream, it's OK, because it was an accident. Pretty sure.

***

I had the rare opportunity on Good Friday this year to take a quick road trip with our daughter to Bozeman, Montana to pick up her son. We left Pocatello around 2:30 and Nique started as designated driver. She let me take the helm in Ashton, Idaho and we headed through West Yellowstone and up Gallatin Canyon. As I was driving through Big Sky, Montana at only 45 mph, things changed for the worst. As we approached Big Sky Road where it connects to the highway, the light at the intersection turned from green to yellow. Nowadays my mind doesn't work very fast, and it took a little time to register (kinda like a computer with a virus). When I saw the light change, everything went into slow motion. It went from yellow to red pretty fast while I was still in the process of debating whether to smash down on the gas or not. My once cat-like reflexes had me hit the brakes and a gallon jug of drinking water sitting on the back seat on the driver side slid straight forward, smashing the back of my seat with the force of a German Shepard. The cap of the jug popped off and shot water straight up to the ceiling! That is when I was baptized right there on the spot. The jug then fell upside down on our jackets which had taken a trip to the floor. Nique reached back as fast as she could to save our jackets from a good soakin', but the jug had already gotten in two good glugs. Our jackets were soaked but we were OK.

Once we had cell service, we found out that the guys (her son and his dad) were having trouble with their truck. It was pukin' transmission fluid all over and they were only in Sheridan, Wyoming. So, when we got to Bozeman, we filled with gas and headed towards Billings to meet them there. When we finally met them it was 22 degrees out, the wind was blowing, and it started to snow. We went to Shopko, bought new jackets, had a nice dinner and headed towards home.

Our daughter was in the driver's seat again in a whiteout and driving 35 mph. I helped by watching reflector poles along the road and thanked Jesus that we weren't driving by braille. By the time we got to Livingston she had had enough. We traded drivers and off we went again. I stopped to fill with gas in Belgrade and got a cup of "coffee" to help keep me awake. Nastiest stuff I have ever had the privilege of stickin' in my mouth. I didn't have the time to take my hands off the steering wheel to cut the stuff up. We made it past the baptism spot at about 2 a.m., but this time there were only deer and elk there. We managed to get home by 6 a.m. What a trip!

Good times I reckon!!!

***

I will know when my time here on earth is about up when I don't have the air to blow hard enough to separate two coffee filters.

Gee whiz. Looks like I'm good for another day.

***

I have no idea why women in my family would rather throw somethin' than to get up and go take care of a problem.

I remember my dad telling me that grandma did it as well. One day he was doing somethin' naughty while grandma was puttin' some clothes away, and instead of going after him, she threw the only thing that was handy at the time... which was a girdle laying on the bed. Dad started to run but he said that thing tied him up and gave him a beatin' at the same time.

I have witnessed this same thing for the last 63 years... the female human doesn't waste time or energy chasin' stuff. Our son had a habit of mouthin' off while standing far enough away from my wife, Georgia. This started at a young age when he was only about 5 years old. He thought he would put this little mouthy thing he had into practice. Georgia was doing somethin' in the living room, I think she was sitting on the floor changin' Nique's diaper when little mouthy-mouth proceeds to announce his dissatisfaction about somethin'. He knew that by the time mom got up to slap the snot out of him, he could lock himself in the bathroom or get out the front door until things calmed down. One thing he didn't realize was that his dad had married a woman that could qualify for starting quarterback for the Denver Broncos. So, the little stinker started mouthin' off this fine summer day as he stood in front of the door with it open so he could make a clean getaway. Georgia grabbed the closest object...one of Stan's tennis shoes. She launched that sucker and hit little "mouth" square in the forehead and knocked him ass-over-teacup out the front door. I didn't get to witness this little incident but was informed when I came home from work.

I have seen things fly that had not been in the atmosphere before. My sister used to do that a lot when I was growing up. Now I know why she did it. It wasn't because she couldn't catch me when she thought she needed to give me a beatin', but because I was in training for my future. I think the only thing Jason learned from Georgia's training sessions was... to DUCK. Yup!!! When he was in high school, he took another shot at it. When I arrived home after work, Georgia proceeded to inform me about Jason mouthin' off again. A book was apparently the nearest tool, but this time Jason had successfully learned to duck... and so the book crashed through the winda'. I guess glass wasn't that expensive.

Yup!!! Good Times.

***

Georgia had a meeting up at the gun range and left me in charge of supper. I know it's simple and not rocket science, and Stan is in charge. I decided on some frozen hot dogs wrapped in dough'. Yup!!! Preheat oven to 400, spray a baking sheet with a non-stick substance, load the pan, put in oven for 20 to 22 min. Just to make sure, I allowed them to cook the full 22 min. It did NOT say where the stupid rack in the oven was supposed to be so, when my 22 minutes were up, I pulled them out. And instead of little baked hot dogs in golden dough, I wound up with chunks of charcoal in a hockey puck.

***

Some people think they are pretty smart but sometimes it comes back to haunt them.

So this someone caught a spider with a rag and then threw the spider in the toilet and flushed it. Spiders can float I reckon, so... it floated back up. So that somebody pushed him down to the bottom of the toilet with a toilet plunger. But apparently, spiders can hold their breath for a long period of time... at least as long as it takes to have two cups of coffee and a couple donuts!

I removed the toilet plunger, and that spider was still hangin' on to it!!! I bounced him back in the toilet and threw a piece of toilet paper over him thinking it would hold him down and I could flush him down that way. But he just turned over and walked under the toilet paper and up on top of it like he had just finished building the raft himself. I can't seem to get rid of this chunk of walkin' Velcro and it's takin' its toll on my patience. I have been tryin' to get rid of this thing for a couple hours now. I jam that toilet plunger down on him and push up and down so fast and hard it sucks all the oxygen out of the bathroom. I hit the flush knob and standby, ready to whack him with the plunger if he shows his face again.

Silly spider! I should have stomped him in the first place, and I wouldn't have had to grab my oxygen hose to get my air back. Talk about a workout!

***

Sooooo... My wife has a sweet tooth tonight. I know because she told me to go to the store and buy something "DISGUSTING", like a cake or donuts or somethin'.

***

Not too long ago, I had the privilege of staying in a place for a few days that had the prices of the Hotel Hilton without the service. I can say that you don't get any sleep there even though Bob Boudet left the light on for ya, so it couldn't have been Motel 6. Now these new hospitals have everything available to make your body work. If they have a body, they don't care if it's a good one or not, they can get that sucker workin'. Let me tell you about a couple things I ran across there. They have this do-dad that is like a Mallard duck bill at one end and I was told that the object was to blow through, and it would make you cough. I normally try to get things to make me quit coughin', so this one is new to me. I blew on that Mallard and it did... it made me cough. I had some stuff in my lungs that I couldn't cough up, so this was going to help me clear that stuff out. So, my instructor said when I needed to cough some of this up and get it out of my system, I was to grab the Mallard and blow 6 or 8 times. Well, I'm in this place BECAUSE I can't breathe, and now they want me to waste what little air I have blowing on a Mallard? By the time I blow on that sucker and cough enough, I don't have the air to cough anything up. I keep gasping for air and the nurse givin me instructions is saying, "You need to take bigger breaths and blow them out all the way out, so you empty your lungs completely." It just doesn't make sense. If you are in my shape, you want to save just a little of that oxygen, just in case you need it. I never did cough anything up, but they let me keep the dead Mallard, just in case. I think I made some new friends there. They seemed to have a good time.

Yup!!! Good Times.

***

I know that you can accomplish anything if you put your mind to it. Two of the hardest things I have ever done: quit smoking and open one of those big no-name bags of cheerios.

***

The other day, I had a not-so-good experience with our local hospital. I guess the experience was okay, I just definitely don't want to do it again. You know how hospitals are... it doesn't matter what is wrong with you, they hand you a little gown, with no back on it and say "you can keep your shorts on, but put this on". Well, I think at the price they charge for a night's stay, you should get a gown with a back in it. Now I'm havin' problems breathin' and they have all kinds of things to help. They have this machine; I think the nurse called it a C cups or somethin'. I know when we go into Costco, I look for K cups for our coffee maker, and Georgia looks for another size cup for some clothes, but the nurse insists that this thing has nothing to do with coffee or a #*@. It has a mask that they want to strap over and seal against my face. Now this thing practically breathes for you. If you breathe out, it replaces the air you let out and sometimes it doesn't mess around. So, I'm sitting up in bed and the nurse is trying to get this sucker strapped on me, so that it seals good. She is telling me how it works, and the thing blows a puff of air every time I breathe out. She's asking questions and I try to answer, but every time I do it shoots me a mouth full air. Well, it got to be funny. Every time I would smile or giggle, I'd get a shot of air. I had a little air leak on my chin and so when I grinned, it shot a puff of air, went right down the front of that two-bit skirt they gave me, tickled the hair on my chest, all the way down to my navel, and damn near blew my shorts off!! I think it would have if I had not been sittin' at the time. Now my grandpa used to do that, but didn't need a machine and the air didn't come from his face.

They really wanted me to sleep all night with this thing on. I wondered what would be left on the shelves in the morning if they thought they could trust me with one of those. So just a reminder, make sure your underwear has good elastic if you have to use the C cup machine. I think if I have to again, I'm bringing my own suspenders.

Yup!!! Good Times, well kinda.

***

Why is it that when your granddaughter splits a donut with you and it comes out 1/3 and 2/3, and she hands you the little one, you say, "Looks even to me."

***

Well, I had a hearing test done yesterday. The results... I think she said I can't hear much. They cannot do anything with one ear because it's so bad. I took that to mean that in order to get enough power for a hearing aid, I'd have to tote a 12-volt car battery around. But a hearing aid will apparently help the other ear. I think she said I would be surprised to know what I have been missing. (I got all that in writing.) But I'm not going to do a hearing aid, not yet anyway, those suckers are expensive.

So, for anyone I have talked to in the last 2 or 3 years, that is the reason I sat on your lap while we talked and kept saying, "Eh?" I will not tell anyone which ear I can't hear out of so you can't put the sneak on me from behind. Good news is I can still see! Well, as long as I have ears to hold my glasses on with.

***

One day last week, Georgia and her sister Patti went shopping at Winco for some groceries. Those two get together and talk a lot and other (important) details kinda go out the winda'. They had bought a few things and were talking at the back of the car with the back hatch open. Their next stop being about a block away, they hopped on the main road and when they got to Walgreens, noticed that the back hatch was still open! So somewhere between Walgreens and Winco, there is a head of lettuce and a couple notebooks.

Sometimes you wish lettuce was square.

***

Sooo, I was just wondering about those lunch meat companies that have the really, really, thin sliced turkey breast and ham and stuff. Why in the world do they slice that so stinkin' thin? Do people think they are getting a good deal if it says 76 pieces and do they still sell it by the pound? Who in the world would put one slice of meat on a sammich' anyway? It takes 6 pieces before you can't see the bread through the meat for cryin' out loud!... then another 6 for flavor!

One time we went to Illinois to Georgia's sister's house and stayed a week or so.

If I remember right, Georgia's sister Patti was getting married. Georgia's other sister Sherron was there and her husband Joe and their cousin Barbara. We are all getting ready for a big dinner and everyone is doing something to get ready. Someone is cutting the meat; someone is making salad. Everyone is doing something to help, except Barb. Now Barb really tries to do some things, but she is busy samplin' stuff as well. She does a little and samples a lot and does a little and samples some more. But everyone is so busy doing their own thing, that the only one seeing Barb sampling stuff is good ole Stan. Now Sherron and Joe have this old diabetic cat that they haul around because it has to have a shot every day, so when they go somewhere, the cat goes with them. Joe decides he is going to feed the cat so he doesn't later get side tracked and forget. So, he has a paper plate and opens a can of cat food, empties it on the plate, cuts it up some and heads for the refer for something.

Well, Barb didn't see this happen with the cat food, but Stan did. He just stood off to the side to see this thing go down. He is pretty sure this is going to be cool. Barb turned around and... hey, there is somethin' new that she hasn't sampled yet! Looks like some kind of fish stuff and smells kinda good. Now I think that Barb thinks this is some kind of super luxury stuff. So, taking her handy dandy fork... she tries a bite. Boy, I really thought she was going to spew! She went through all the motions, and even did the little sound effects and even made it to the garbage to spit that crap out without anyone seeing or hearing her! Well, everyone except Stan, who looked the other way when she looked around to see if anyone saw her. I had to make my way into the bathroom to laugh, because this was going to be a big deal when the time is right. So, we were all at the dinner table eating and Barbara said, "Oh this ham is just great!" Yup... you guessed it! This was Stan's cue. Now Stan normally is pretty soft spoken, kinda low keyed. But this time, he couldn't help blurting out loud and clear, "A lot better than the cat food you had earlier, Barb?" Barbara was so good about it. She said, "Oh gosh I was hoping no one saw that." I said, "I know you did." So, I had to tell everyone what happened, and everyone had a great laugh.

Yup!!! Good Times.

* * *

I went to pick up some prescriptions today and while I was gone, my wife left work to go straight to Inkom and tried to call me at home from the road. She has this do-dad in the car and all she has to do is touch somethin' and say out loud, "Call Stan," and then the car calls me at home. What the heck? Well, the car called and since I wasn't home, our house answered. But evidently, the house didn't want to talk to the car and hung up on it. Now my wife is upset at the house for hangin' up on her car. We are in serious trouble!

THE CAR

This shows you how lazy we are getting.... One used to have to go out to physically start your car. But now you can sit in front of the living room window and start it. Heck, you can even unlock the doors from there and even open the hatchback. While driving, there is even a green light on the dash that tells you there is a car in front of you. If you approach said car too fast... the dash lights up red and sirens go off. Then, if your wife doesn't do it, that lady somewhere in the car will give you an ass chewin'! The car buzzer will tell when you are drifting across the white line, and also has yellow lights on the side mirrors that tell you when a car is beside you. Now apparently we have more time to keep our eyes on our phone so we can text instead of paying attention to driving.

I tried to send our car out for a hamburger the other day. I waited 30 minutes and the dang thing just sat out there with the engine running. What the hell?

There's also a TV on the dash so you don't have to look behind while backing up. I reckon it's too much exercise to turn your head a little. Once driving, we don't even have to reach over and lock our doors anymore, the stinkin' car does that for you. You can also tell the car to call someone, and it does.

I guess we have an old-fashioned car, because we still have to turn our windshield wipers on by hand, but my sister-in-law's car will turn them on if the windshield gets a little wet. My gosh. Our wiper switch has 67 settings on the steering column and behind the steering wheel. I'm afraid I'll get yelled at if I lean over to look. There are so many settings on the radio menu. I guess that's why I thought the car could go get me a hamburger. I was kinda waiting to see if it asked me if I wanted "fries with that".

Our car has a switch on the seat that adjusts everything in the car to customize to whoever is sitting in the seat. I guess it's afraid you're going to forget to adjust somethin'. One thing I can't get used to is the windows. Push a button, they go down, but you have to stick your finger in a little hole and pull up on the switch to get it to go up. Are they worried that with a rocker button, your dog is going to step on it and choke himself or maybe your kid? I didn't see anything wrong with the old manual window crank, can't remember anyone gettin' choked by them.

On to the all-in-one do-dad steering wheel and computer. This thing has everything on the horn ring... except the horn. If it has a horn... I can't find it. You can control your speed, up and down, turn on stuff that says ya' don't have to look where you're going, answer your phone, turn your radio up and down. The headlights even know when it's dark and turn on by themselves. You don't even have to dim them anymore... seems they know when a car is comin'.

To top it all off, most of the car is now plastic. So, we have a smart-ass Tupperware car. Probably the best transportation ever is a horse and buggy or a bicycle. Can you imagine the exercise you'd get? Might put a lot of people out of work though. I guess I'm finished.

***

Boy, this stinkin' computer is so dang slow and it takes so long for a page to come up, I either forgot what I clicked for or I fall asleep waiting. Holy Smokes!

Hope I can get it fixed soon. Then I can join my FB friends again.

***

HELLO EVERYONE: Yes, I am still here. You guys hang in there, I will try not to get out of control. I am writing for one main reason, but I thought of another while trying to write the first reason. Well, now I dang near forgot the first one. Here it is. We only have three 1971 class calendars left if some of you would like one. Only 10 bucks, or 13 bucks if we need to ship it to you. Now these suckers are pretty cool and handmade. We are going to have a new year, ya know, pretty soon. Sooooo, if you can't live without one of these super great, handmade class calendars with 13 pages of glory and pictures of people, let us know and we will hook you up. The second reason is to remind everyone about Ruthie's Highland Class of 1971 Christmas Dinner. You guys who haven't been there, don't realize what you're missin'. You get to sit in the living room and kitchen eatin' good food in front of a bunch of classmates. Kinda cool, almost like the lunchroom at school. Ruthie has two little vacuum cleaners that keep stuff off the floor. Actually, nothing ever hits the floor, those little whiz kids get it first. So, please come have some fun with us. There are a lot of stories and laughin' and just good old hometown fun goin' on. It is Dec. 13th. Everyone needs to enjoy this at least once. You won't regret it, I'm pretty sure. Just so you know, I'm not like this in person. Sorry, I got out of control again. See what Georgia has to deal with? Come and have some fun with us.

***

Ya know, at least once every couple of days I have a sneezin' fit. I sneeze about 6 times in a row. I do not have an excess amount of oxygen to be puttin' on a performance like this all the time. When I **ah, ah, ah! ...choo!!!** 5 times in a row, I'm already gettin' pretty short on oxygen and have to do some pantin' and gaspin' for air to keep me breathin'. It's always on the 6th "ah, ah, ah..." that I have to work pretty hard and at the end, I only get a little tiny... "choo!" And that pisses me off!

***

As we get older, it amazes me how much our childhood antics return to us. Like, setting a piece of your Happy Birthday cake on a paper plate with your fork handle stickin' off the edge. You leave it on the arm of your rocker recliner, misjudging how long that fork handle really is and when you sit down, your britches catch the fork handle and it launches your Happy Birthday cake out into the middle of the living room. Yup!! Brings back good old memories.

Callantine Family Reunion

Ya' know, when we get older some of us still think like kids.

We had a family reunion a couple weeks ago. Cousins came from Texas and Washington, along with my nephew, Michael Callantine. Donna Flores, and Deniece Wilson Morgan, are all girls, and pretty cool ones at that.

We go to a cemetery where a lot of our relatives are buried out in the foothills. I'm being the guide because I remember stuff. I heard a rumor that there might be rattlesnakes in there, so I grab my pistol. Now, I have COPD, so I kinda operate a little slower than most, but everyone is cool with that. When we pull up we notice on the gate it reads in big black letters "NO SHOOTING". One of my cousins said, "No shooting Stan, now what?" Now I know I need to keep the girls safe, kinda makes a feller feel important. I think the girls call it "showin' off." With my quick thinkin', I say, "I reckon I'll have to pistol whip 'em. Yup! I'll save ya." The girls are in and out of the cemetery before I get halfway in. "We're Done." No snakes.

So off to Maudlow we go to our grandpa's house. I told the girls it's "just up the road a ways". Well, I don't think the girls are used to goin "just up the road a ways". After a little while, we stop so I can walk back to point out a few deer that I'm sure the girls will miss if I don't show 'em. When they ask how much farther it is, I confirm, "Just up the road a ways." Well, it was just up the road a little farther than I thought, but you don't want to tell the girls that. Heck, they might think ya don't know nothin'. We finally make it and walk around, up the road to the bridge that crossed the creek.

On the way back, Mikey, my daughter and I are ridin' in the jeep and as we pass the girls, I'm pretty sure I hear a bloody scream along with my name. "THERE IS A SNAKE, STAN."

Mikey slams on the brakes, gravel flyin' and dust fills the air. Before the Jeep stops, my door opens, and I bail out to save my lovely cousins. With my catlike reflexes, I jump between the girls and the snake. Now this is where COPD and adrenaline don't get along. I can see the snake clearly now, but my hands are on my knees and I'm bent over tryin' to catch my breath as the snake slithers like greased lightning right there in front of me. (I had gone the full length of the Jeep before restin'.) I can't hear Mikey from all the screamin' goin' on, but after I stop screamin', I get a little shot of oxygen. When I catch up to the snake, I need a little rest and realize I left my pistol in the Jeep! This snake crawled so fast he left a trail of dust behind him. I had to let him go. By the time I could get my pistol the snake would have crossed into Canada. But I'm pretty sure that 10-inch garter snake learned a lesson.

I think the girls really wanted to see me pistol whip that snake though. This is what they had said, "HEY STAN, PISTOL WHIP THIS." Kinda funny how things sound different in the clear mountain air of Montana. I have the best cousins in the world!

Thank you, Donna Flores, Linda Tang, Deniece Wilson Morgan, Nique Callantine and Michael Callantine for the great memories. I will never forget the fun we have.

Yup!!! Good Times.

***

You know your hair is thinnin' a little bit when you get out of the shower and your hair is dry by the time you dry yourself off. Yup!! Both of them.

***

A month ago, my wife and I bought a couple of kayaks. Oh, what fun when yesterday we finally got to try them out. There are a few things you want to take into consideration whilst thinkin' about buying one of these things. 1) What is your age? 2) Can you swim? 3) Do you have pretty good balance? 4) Can you catch yourself on slippery stuff? 5) What is your oxygen level? 6) Can you get up off a flat surface? Tell you what, we had a good time...I think.

If an old couple sits flat on the floor for a couple hours, then tries to stand up on a basketball half full of oxygen so they can step on a wet sheet of ice carrying a paddle... and a fishin' pole, something has gotta give. That is what it is like getting out of a kayak from the water and over to a muddy bank. We saved the kayaks from takin' off without us fthough, thanks to my wife's genius suggestion of tying a little rope on them before we left. Managed to get everything stuffed back in the truck and home safe. Holy smokes does everything hurt! As I rolled over in bed about 3:00 AM, if someone had offered me a song and a dance for a couple kayaks, they probably would have had a deal. This afternoon I am still sore, but I have come to my senses. Maybe if we do this more often, it won't be so bad. I'll have to ask Georgie when she gets off work when we can go again.

***

I have a real bad case of heartburn. I wonder if it's the 73 cups of coffee I had today?

***

Sooo, to fix the earlier heartburn problem, I got one of those Rolaids soft chews that has been in the medicine cabinet for too long. It was still soft, kinda, but when I chomped down on it and went to chomp again, my teeth were stuck to it so I had to spit my teeth out and pry them off the soft chew. Sometimes ya' have to put your Rolaid in the microwave for a minute so you can chew it!

**

Me and that dang car are going to go the rounds if it doesn't stop it. It thinks it's so smart that my opinion doesn't count.

I try to let Georgie out of the car, but the car won't let her out until I put it in park.

I crank the radio up so I can hear it. I stop to go into the store and while I am gone, that stinkin' car turns the radio back down.

I stop in front of the house at night and turn the key off. The dome light stays on, so I start writing a note to myself on a sheet of paper when the light decides to turn off right in the middle of a sentence!

I must be a burr under its saddle or somethin'. Sure is going to feel a little better while Georgie is gone and takes this little creep with her. I'll stick with my not-so-smart pickup truck for a week or so.

**

We had a pretty good trip this last weekend. We were going across Wyoming and the weather was a little nasty. It was dark out and snowin' and blowin'... a real whiteout. Couldn't see very far in front of you. There was a lot of screamin' and stuff for about 20 minutes. That is when Georgia told me to stop it because she couldn't hear the radio.

***

So, I was going to go check out the new Winco store the other day. But, by the time I walked from my parking place to the store, it had taken so long, I had to go back home to eat lunch. I think I'll pack it next time in my Roy Rogers lunch box.

***

My wife and I decided to get a couple of those fancy watches that tell ya' how many calories you've burned, how far you've walked, and what your heart rate is. I had a little trouble with my ticker this last summer and fall, so we thought this would be a great thing to keep tabs on my heartbeat while we are out and about. So we just got them and Georgie set mine up last evening. Well, all I wanted to know was how far I walked and my heart rate. I had about 350 steps in by midnight. Then, instead of turning into a frog at midnight, my watch changed to 0 to start a new day. I wore that thing to bed and when I woke up this mornin', I had 117 steps in already. That can't be right, so I checked. It is exactly 11 steps from my side of the bed to the toilet. I know I made this trip twice. Well, now I'm wonderin' where the rest of those steps came from, so I am checkin' here and there, adding and subtracting and multiplying. I even tried some algebra and geometry but decided I had no idea what I was doin' so I went back to addin' and subtractin'.

Remember those story problems we used to do in school? If Billy had 67 apples and Peggy ate 6, how many apples did Billy have left? I was pretty good at those. I got this now, two trips to the toilet, one trip to the refrigerator, and a trip to Facebook and back to bed added up pretty close. I must have tripped over my oxygen hose somewhere along the way to get the other four steps. So, I have my exercise in for the day. I hope you all have a great day.

When I got my eyes fixed, I had to buy reading glasses, so I went to the dollar store and bought three pair, three weeks ago. LOST-EM. Yup!!! I looked in the fridge, AIN'T THERE.

Well, I was feelin' pretty good yesterday, so I decided to put some steps on my new wristwatch step counter do-dad. I had about 1,200 steps in already. Did you know that you are supposed to walk about 10,000 steps a day? I know that means I'm probably going to have to get out of the house.

Wait...a...min...ute, I have a treadmill!

So, I hopped on the treadmill and headed out on my journey. I was huffin' and puffin' after 1/4 mile, but I'm going for 1/2 mile. I'm so stinkin' proud I look at my step counter watch and it reads exactly the same as when I left. What the heck, if I would have known they didn't count, I would have stayed home. Who would have thought that this thing wouldn't work on a treadmill? I found out through a little research. Well, I asked Jason, and he said there is a sensor in there that works on motion. If I had known that I would have hung onto the bar with only one hand. I just threw 1/2 mile out the window! That is like getting my shirt sleeve caught on the car bumper when Georgie is goin' to the store and I run behind the car without movin' my arm. All those steps wouldn't count. Who says we have to take 10,000 steps anyway? Oh yeah! If you stand in one spot and just swing your arm back and forth, back and forth, back and forth, it doesn't register either. Well, I won't be taken to the cleaners again. I got this.

I was outside for a while and when I came in the house, my wife had fallen asleep in the chair with her cell phone facing up on her lap. It looked like she had a message with just a couple words on it so with my x-ray vision I read, "Love Brittney". We know two people named Brittney. Not trusting my x-ray vision, I got my glasses to get a better look and see which one it was. I didn't want to take the phone for fear it might wake her up. I leaned down closer to the phone, and read, "Low Battery".

Well, that makes sense.

＊

Since I got out of the hospital a week or so ago, I have to be on oxygen all the time. Boy, what a pain in the A$$. You're only good to go as far as your hose will reach. Here is another problem I have...the oxygen hose goes in your nose and up over your ears. Now I'm pretty sure that is not why God gave us ears, but I guess we've found extra uses for them... hangin oxygen hoses and eyeglasses on. So, this morning I was sitting in a chair watchin TV and decided I needed some more coffee, so I grabbed my cup and stood up. Unfortunately, I stood on my oxygen hose and damn near pulled my ears off.

＊

Wreaths on your door during Christmas time look so nice. One thing you need to remember, though... if you have a screen door on your home, the wreath should be on that. It sure makes a mess of those bulbs and pinecones if you have it on the inside door. I will get that mess picked up. Yup!!!! We are still learnin' stuff.

＊

We've had this cute little rabbit hanging around Georgie's garden this summer. Ya know I've fought for that rabbit's wellbeing for about two months now. I even named him Lucky. I went out and bought him a bag of rabbit food and a head of lettuce, gave him carrots and an apple, and one time he even ate a few grapes. I frisked my wife at the back door to make sure she wasn't packin' heat to plaster that little bastard into Kingdom-come if she caught him in her garden again. I put my future, even my home and my marriage on the line for this Lucky little chit.

Ain't laid eyes on him for about a week now so I am assuming I have been taken advantage of once again. Lucky just left... no note or anything. Ungrateful little chit. I searched the neighborhood and every nook and cranny in the yard. You just can't trust anyone anymore. There was a time when you could look a bull in the face and knew that he was going to mop the ground with you. Those days are gone.

Georgia and I used to hunt a lot in our younger days. I would hunt critters because they were destructive and asked her if she would go with me. She told me "Nope, I won't shoot anything I can't eat." I did offer to cook some of that up for her, but she turned it down. Thinking about that, something rang a bell, and I ran downstairs to check the freezer for wild game packages with "Wabbit" written on it. Nope... not there, and we haven't had stew or chicken lately.

I was just about to check into the cost to have him's picture put on a milk carton when I noticed on Facebook that Pocatello Animal Shelter had a bunch of bunnies, but I didn't see Lucky's mug shot in there. Him's just might have gotten picked up by the rabbit police and thrown in the hooshcow.

Just my luck! I don't think I would go pay them for stealing our bunny. I think I will give him another week... you know, just in case he went underground from all the rain. Yikes!!!

***

Bought some of them "Focus Factor" pills a while back. You know the ones that makes ya' remember stuff? Can't remember where I put 'em though. So, instead of wastin' more money on that pill stuff, bought myself one of them fancy memory foam mattresses. Can't say that's workin' either, but I did run across them pills.

***

I'm always learnin' stuff. When I got my eyes fixed, I found out that we had more cats than I thought.

***

Just so ya' know, not even an alley cat is free.

Here is the deal.

If ya hang out at our house too long, you're going to get your shots and probably your propeller pulled. That must be the reason we don't have any friends come over to visit. So, long story short... (surprise!!! Short story.) we wound up at the Humane Society and for our senior citizen discount, a picture of Georgia, Sylvester, and $50, we can keep the stray cat. Just so ya know, the 50 bucks was for shots and getting his propeller pulled. Its official, signed the papers yesterday.

Are we suckers or what? We have free food here, folks, but you might not leave with everything you came with.

***

I swear, one of the hardest things to do before bedtime is to get both of our cats on the same side of the door at once. You let one in and the other goes out. Then you let the one that is in, out, and the one that's out comes in. Then he goes out and the other one comes in.

Good thing my wife bought one of those electric fly swatters at a yard sale a couple weeks ago. Those things really fry the flies.

***

My wife gets up about two hours before I do in the morning. Sometimes I can see that things have been moved, changed from the night before. Some mornings, like yesterday, she is pretty active. Now to understand how this lady thinks, you would have to spend 46 years with her. She is pretty cute inside and out and her thinkin'... well, her thinkin' is pretty cute also.

When I got up and came into the kitchen, I saw a meat grinder on the stove. Then by the coffee pot there was a roll of duct tape and a lot of room on the counter by the fridge. Now folks, nothing I am seein' so far was a good thing. I got my cup of coffee and started investigating the situation and thinkin' about what might have gone on. Well, this is what happened...

***

Remember I told ya the other day that a stray cat had figured out the pet door? Georgie was in the living room having her morning coffee and heard some 'singin' in the kitchen. She went in to find the stray cat inside and our old Xochi cat didn't like it. So, Georgie stomped her feet and yelled at him and he lit out in a flash. So, she proceeded to tear up the kitchen looking for the "no come-in" cover for the pet door, it was nowhere to be found. So, this was where Georgie shined with her en-gine-uity. She set our food processer in front of the door so the flap couldn't open and, just in case that was too light, she set the meat grinder on top for extra weight. My wife is the best. Meanwhile she had gone to the bathroom to curl her hair and heard a bunch of racket and the 'singin' started again. She ran in the kitchen and chased Houdini out again. The cat didn't have quite enough room to get out the door, and I think he went through the meat grinder. So, here is where the duct tape came in... the dustpan was duct taped to the wall where the pet door used to be and the motor to the food processor was in front of that.

I reckon it worked because I haven't seen the cat since yesterday. I am afraid to step outside to see if that cat is stuck to the outside of the pet door. I am also afraid of what I might find duct taped to the boat or the shed if that cat doesn't show up by spring. I LOVE MY GEORGIE.

Yup!!! Good Times.

***

Boy, I'm going to have to get serious about getting new hearing aid batteries. I went to the doctor today and he said we were getting a Cadillac Escalade. I told Georgie, but she told me that he said I need "cataract surgery". Oh well, we can dream, I guess.

***

Sad news today. Gizmo bit the bullet. I don't know if I drowned him, or he had a heat stroke, or what happened. Him's was lookin' a little peaked and a little brown around the edges so I thought he was in too small of a pot. I bought him a brandy new pot and him's sure looked good in blue. He was doing okay for a few weeks, so I decided to take him outside. He never changed and was just there. Our neighbors gave me a pine tree in a plastic bag that Home Depot gave to them. I planted him in the old pot that Gizmo had. He was doing great, so I set him right next to Gizmo and he continued to grow but Gizmo never grew any more. Since he didn't grow, I decided to replant him into a bigger pot which we already had, thinkin' him's roots needed more room. Him's evidently didn't like him's new home. The little pine tree was still growing and doing fine, so I replanted him in Gizmo's blue room.

I am now afraid to name the little pine for fear him's will get sick and die like Gizmo did. I honestly don't know what happened to Gizmo. Sometimes I think he might have died of a broken heart because I helped the little pine tree and gave him Gizmo's old room. Gizmo is just a 10-inch stick now with two leaves at the top that look like little brown paper bags. I am not sure if I should give him a burial or what. I know he probably wouldn't want to be in a pine box, maybe I should make one out of oak for him. Naw, be my luck I would make it out of him's grandpa. I reckon I could just cremate him over the Barbi. Hummmmm!!! That little pine tree is really doing well, I will get some pictures one of these days. I guess I will name him. I will call him Knotty.

Yup!!! Knotty Pine! :) Or how about Turpen?

So how about it you guys, should I name him, Knotty Pine or Turpen Pine??

***

I've been gettin' in shape over the last week. I think I would do a little better if I replace the Little Debbie's cherry pies I keep in the pockets on the treadmill with my three pound dumbbells. I was also thinkin' I might pull my exercise bike away from the back of the treadmill, so the tire isn't tight against the treadmill track. I did notice when the treadmill was runnin' it was spinnin' the tire on the exercise bike but didn't pay much attention until I got off my exercise bike yesterday to get another cookie. When I came back my bike had put on 57 miles. Thank the Lord for coaster brakes on my exercise bike. I reckon I now know why I don't get so tired while ridin' my exercise bike and I get wore out walkin' to the car.
...I'm just joshin' ya, I don't have an exercise bike.

***

I'll tell you what, you must have a great sense of humor livin' around us. I went through my daily ritual lookin' for where I laid my glasses the last time, usually a 15 to 30 minute escapade. Then I sat down to take a break and watch TV for a bit. Georgie came in and said, "Oh!! There it is, I couldn't find the coon." Well, you know how great my hearing is, so of course I thought she was talkin' about Puddy Tat, our big old outside cat so I said, "I think he's outside." She replied, "I said, 'Oh there it is, I couldn't find the vacuum'." We live such a wonderful goofy life, you guys don't know what you're missin'.

***

According to fitbit, I earned my Penguin Marching badge yesterday. I must have really impressed them with my walking skills. I'm not even sure penguins have knees, their legs are so short. Wonder how many steps I got?

***

Was makin' some toast this mornin' and found a little tiny brown bug on the counter. I took my butter knife and chased it around in front of the toaster for a while before I was able to pin him down. Every time I would push the handle of my butter knife on his back, he would shoot out, the slick little bugger. I held my finger in front of him so he couldn't take off and got the job done. Smashed him flat as a piece of paper right there in front of the toaster. I checked him out since it looked like his insides were now on his outside. He turned out to be a seed off of a piece of bread Georgie had toasted earlier. Happy Days!!!

***

It's kinda nice today, so I was doin' some spring cleanin'. Cleanin' out the fridge, I ate quite a bit of stuff and came across a jar of Granny's Sizzlin' Salsa. Now this stuff was kinda green and kinda brown, pretty runny on one side of the jar, but kinda sticky on the other side. I had to pry the lid off with my wife's favorite screwdriver (a butter knife). I decided to clean the toilet with that salsa and man, does our toilet look brand new again!

I wish I knew where we got that stuff and how long we had to age it in the fridge. I bet we could market it as a toilet cleaning solution and be rich. I would even donate a jar to the "Museum of Clean". Yup! It's okay to keep the American dream alive.

***

Boy! I have got to hand it to ladies that can do more than one thing at once. Georgie makes it look easy.

I was trying to do that, multi-task, whilst makin' my lunch... some ramen noodles and a spam sammich. Well, that went over like a screen door on a submarine. I got my noodles out of the package and started heating up the water whilst making my sammich. I got everything out and my sammich was now almost ready. I only had to slice spam to put on it for it to be done. Now where did I put those stinkin' noodles? I know good and well I didn't leave the kitchen with them. By the time I found them, almost all the water boiled out. I forgot that I had pulled my spam out of the fridge. I guess I had put the pack of noodles down somewhere to pick up the spam. Yes!! Somebody put the noodles in the fridge.

I am such a dork, can't imagine what life would be like if I was normal.

***

I did some multi-tasking today. Yup!!!! I sneezed, farted and peed my pants. Gettin' old has its' problems.

***

Cleaned up the BBQ tonight... was gonna barbeque some hamburgers. The grill had been sittin' out all winter and seems as though the igniter decided it's still winter, so I pulled the grates off and turned the gas on just a little. Where did I lay those matches? Oh yeah, here we go. I better turn the gas off for a little while. There, that should be long enough. Nope!! Needed a little more time. Got me a sunburn, shave and a haircut in about .300 of a second and saved me a hundred bucks. Sure smelled bad for a minute, almost ruined my appetite :)

***

Went through Yellowstone Park last Sunday. Came home empty handed, couldn't get a buffalo in the car.

***

We took our kayaks down fishin' yesterday. The reservoir has a lot of mud along the banks, and it is a trip trying to get in and out of a kayak. Our kayaks have a somewhat concave bottom to make them more stable in the water. After being in mine for an hour or so, I'm ready to get out and stretch. Some body parts just don't work like they used to. So, I paddle my kayak up in front of the dam because the most solid ground is there. I have learned that you shouldn't stand up in a kayak or canoe, but how in the heck do you dismount without standing up a little? I am now parallel with the bank and decide to get on my knees on the seat. That way, I'm at least halfway up just in case somethin' happens. So, I throw my fishin' pole, tackle, and paddle up on the shore. The kayak is now sitting on the bottom in about 2 inches of water and pretty steady, at least on the side closest to the bank. I start to put one foot on the seat but now the line tied to the front of the kayak is wrapped around my ankle and I can't stand. I'll just... nope, I guess I won't use the paddle because I threw it up on the bank. (Sometimes people don't think well under pressure.) I try to unwrap the line without sitting back down. I am just slippin' it under my toe when some things start to wiggle a little. I musta' over corrected. The next thing I know, the six inches of water on the other side of the kayak is now in my hip pocket. I have my life jacket on and I damn near get it wet. If I wasn't sitting on the bottom in waist level water, that thing would have saved my life! The kayak had turned over and flipped a couple of surprised 1" bass up onto the bank. Sure had packed my pockets full of mud and moss.

Georgie came running over to help her oxygen-deprived husband. My dear wife brought a change of clothes and offered me the pants she was wearing while she changed into some cut-offs.

It was still fun even though I tried to deep six myself.

Yup!!! Good Times.

***

I just realized that I wear white T-shirts a lot because at the end of the day, I play a game I call 'Watzat'. I look in the mirror before going to bed and try to guess what it was that missed my mouth here and what squirted out there and what it was that hit my belly before bouncing down between the cushion on the chair. I'm getting pretty good at it. Sometimes I have to taste test it. Yikes!!!! Just doesn't take much to entertain me anymore. That might be a good thing. I'll have to ask Georgia.

***

Dear funeral homes,

Please stop sending me those letters in the mail every week wanting me to make arrangements for my funeral. It is really depressing that it seems to make your day that I might die within the next week or so. It certainly does not make my day go any better. I sure hope that if I don't die soon, your business will not go down the drain. Since I did not die 10 years ago, and I had a great chance of doin' so, it means that God wants me here for the long haul. Please save your stamps and I am sure my wife will contact you when the time comes. There will be no casket, though, so please don't try to sell her one on my account. She has instructions to have my body cremated, pour my ashes in a zip lock bag and drop it in a post hole somewhere in Montana. You folks have a nice day. :)
Sincerely yours,

Stan Callantine

***

Ya know, as time moves on and I get a little older, I have found out that you really can hide stuff from yourself on purpose and get away with it. :) Who knew!!!!!

***

Yesterday, I had a hankerin' for some of mom's good old raisin cookies. Found mom's recipe and started mixin' away. Decided to double the batch. Sometimes it's a good thing to check and make sure you have everything it calls for. This is the first thing I learned. It's not a good idea to put the raisins in and then use your mixer. This is the second thing I learned. Turned my raisin cookies into mincemeat cookies. My mom didn't say how long to leave the cookies in the oven or at what

204

temperature. I'll guess 325 degrees for 8 minutes. This is the third thing. That batch was pretty chewy. Maybe I'll try 350 degrees for 8 minutes. I don't know why I was stuck on the 8-minute thing.

I don't remember mom's cookies lookin' like you could lay one on the newspaper and still read the paper without a glitch or like a deck of playing cards if ya stacked them up. Heck, you can put 20 dozen of these in a sammich bag. Once in a while there would be a bump in one. Guess a few of the raisins made it through the chipper shredder just fine.

I think Georgie felt sorry for me because I was trying so hard. She did something with my cookie dough and they fluffed up a little bit. It took me 4 hours to get them all baked. Slid a couple of them under the microwave to level it up.

Hey! They taste great and look like frisbees.

Yup!!! Good Times.

***

About 4 or 5 times a week, I convince myself that of all the tools in the shed, I'm not the sharpest one.

I have to have oxygen if I'm walking very far on the treadmill, like from one end to the other. You have no idea how far that is. I've been tryin' to get there for the last four years off and on. (More off than on.) I use a rubber band to hold my oxygen hose to the handrail on the treadmill. I get my water, put on my oxygen and the Oldies and I'm on a trip down Memory Lane. This treadmill is one that has the fancy touchpad do-dad dash there in front of you. Oh yeah! It has that magnet and cord that you hook to your britches. An EMERGENCY SHUT-OFF SWITCH, like somethin's gonna happen.

I decided to take our treadmill for a spin this morning. I set my course and took off at 1 mph for about 20 seconds. I stepped it up a little, 2 mph. That's a good speed for me since I am just starting to do this again. I noticed that I left a clean spot where I had touched the buttons to set the machine. So to keep from stopping, I took a Kleenex out of my pocket and dumped a little water on it. Ha, that was a trick! I started wiping the dust off the dash. Folks, this was the wrong thing to do. I wiped over a lot of buttons that change stuff. Before I knew it, I was at a full gallop, climbin' Mount Everest and flippin' water all over everything. I had hit the end of my oxygen hose and damn near pulled my ears off. I thank the Lord for shoelaces. I can't imagine where my shoes would have ended up. I think I kicked myself in the back of the head as I clung to that railing, "just in case somethin' happens." I felt a tug on my britches and then my whole world stopped. Holy Smokes! I think I'll skip tomorrow's walk. I am really tired.

Yup!!! Good Times.

***

About two times a week I get a phone call from Michelle telling me she can lower the interest rates on my credit cards. She said this is my final notice and then says, "Press 1 to speak to a customer service person or press 3 to be taken off our call list". I keep pressing 3 and she keeps calling back. I might be a little slow, but I still get a little oxygen up to my brain, so I am not completely dumb yet.

I think she keeps calling to see if I have gotten off the oxygen!

***

My mom loved to decorate and wrap gift packages. I spent most of yesterday and today wrapping Christmas gifts for our grandkids and family. I don't seem to have my mom's talent. I think you should disguise stuff, so the receiver has no idea what is in the package. Mom was really good at that... she could put a bicycle in a shoe box! I tried for a little while, but I'm not so hot at it. Gosh, at times, it was like tryin' to shove a wet noodle in a straw. My lack of patience and, at times, a vocabulary of choice words when things don't go as well as I think they should, gets me in trouble quite often. I think I've done a good job this year. At least the cats are still in the house.

***

When it rains a little and then starts snowin' those big fat flakes and it gets a little colder and the flakes turn into smaller flakes and the wind blows, we now have a blizzard. Then it stops after a bunch of hours and the temperature drops way down. So, do you know what this means? Yup... a lot of exercise.

I went to the store to get some milk and buns for dinner. Holy Smoke!! I stepped out of the car onto a sheet of ice with a little snow over it. Do you know what that is like? I wished I had had my fitbit on. I ran, skidded, jumped, skipped and shook and I hadn't even turned loose of the car door yet! The keys that were in my hand somehow made it back into the driver's seat. I think that happened when I thought I was going to do an inspection of the muffler system of the car next to me. I can tell you how good the tires are on the cars parked in the general vicinity of my parkin' spot. I'm so stinkin' tired now I don't think I can get into the store for the cauliflower and beef broth I was after.

I did come to my senses and snagged a shoppin' cart to help get me to the store. Oh yeah!!!! Milk and buns. Yup!!!! Still learnin' stuff.

***

This is so funny, I changed a few words, but you can add your own where "friggin'" is. Read on for a SNOW ODYSSEY...

SNOW ODYSSEY 1 - Moved to our new home in Idaho. It is so beautiful here. The mountains are so majestic. Can hardly wait to see them with snow covering them. I love it here.

SNOW ODYSSEY 2 - Idaho is the most beautiful place on Earth. The leaves have turned colors, shades of red and orange. Went for a ride through the beautiful mountains and saw some deer. They are so graceful... certainly they are the most wonderful animal on earth. This must be Paradise. I love it here.

SNOW ODYSSEY 3 - Deer season will start soon. I can't imagine anyone wanting to kill such a gorgeous creature. Hope it will snow soon. I love it here.

SNOW ODYSSEY 4 - It snowed last night. Woke up to find everything blanketed with white. It looks like a postcard. We went outside and cleaned the snow off the steps and shoveled the driveway. We had a snowball fight (I won), and when the snowplow came by, we had to shovel the driveway again. What a beautiful place. I love Idaho!

SNOW ODYSSEY 5 - More snow last night. I love it. The snowplow did his trick again to the driveway. I love it here.

SNOW ODYSSEY 6 - More snow last night. Couldn't get out of the driveway to get to work. I am exhausted from shoveling snow. Damn snowplow.

SNOW ODYSSEY 7 - More of that white shit fell last night. I've got blisters on my hands from shoveling. I think the snowplow hides around the curve and waits until I'm done shoveling the driveway. Asshole!

SNOW ODYSSEY 8 - Merry Friggin' Christmas! More friggin' snow. If I ever get my hands on that son-of-a-bitch who drives that snowplow, I swear I'll kill the bastard. Don't know why they don't use more salt on the roads to melt that damn ice.

SNOW ODYSSEY 9 - More white shit last night. Been inside for three days except for shoveling out the driveway after that snowplow goes through. Can't go anywhere, car's stuck in a mountain of white shit. The weatherman says to expect another 10" of it again tonight. Do you know how many shovels full of snow 10" is?

SNOW ODYSSEY 10 - That damn weatherman was wrong. We got 34" of that white shit this time. At this rate it won't melt before next summer. The snowplow got stuck up the road and that bastard came to the door and asked to borrow my shovel. After I told him I had broken six shovels already shoveling all the shit he pushed into my driveway, I broke my last one over his friggin' head!

SNOW ODYSSEY 11 - Finally got out of the house today. Went to the store to get food and on the way back a damned deer ran in front of the car and I hit it. Did about $3,000 damage to the car. Those beasts should be killed. Wish the hunters had killed them all last November.

SNOW ODYSSEY 12 - Took the car to the garage in town. Would you believe the thing is rusting out from all that damn salt they put all over the road?

SNOW ODYSSEY 13 - Moved to Arizona. I can't imagine why anyone in their right mind would ever live in that God-forsaken state of Idaho!!

Holy Smoke, I went in to get a cup of coffee, looking out the window and right there in the tree in the yard was a little girl squirrel as far out on a limb as she could get and a little boy squirrel just waiting halfway down the limb so she would have to climb past him instead of jumping for safety. Now I know what 'out on a limb' means. Anyway, she managed to get past him but when she got a hold of the tree trunk, he was all over her like white on rice. She just gave up and let him have his way with her. I couldn't handle the porn, so I jumped out the back door and hollered, "HEY CUT THAT OUT!" I don't think I was quick enough. Those little girls should wear britches. :)

Yup!! We are learnin' stuff!!

***

Old Man's birthday: Have you ever thought how when we get older, our eyesight gets bad and we really could use it now since we don't move as fast as we used to. Same thing with our hearing, sure could use that now as well, might just save our bacon. Speaking of bacon, everything seems to smell like bacon when you get old. Or how about our sense of touch? You fall outside and it doesn't hurt until you get in the house even though you look like you went through a chipper shredder and survived.

Now some older folks don't breathe very well and are on oxygen. It just doesn't make sense that some old fella bends over a table with a cake that has 80+ candles and tries to blow them all out. He thinks it smells like bacon and looks like a campfire and he can't hear people yellin' at him that the hair on his arm is on fire. He is too close to the candles because he needs all the oxygen he can get to blow them all out. Do ya' see what's fixin' to happen? He might blow them all to kingdom come. Yup!!!! That is the reason old folks only have one or two at their birthday party.

What an experience!

I got an egg dyeing kit a couple days ago. Now if I remember correctly from back when I was about 10, you need a little vinegar to get started. Looky here! The box turns into an egg drying rack. One thing they do nowadays that is better than when I was little is that they seal stuff really well. By the time I got this box with the kit opened, and the circles on the back punched out, it looked like I opened it with the blender. Well, who needs a drying rack anyway? I had my 6 color tablets in six different cups on the counter with my teaspoon of vinegar to dissolve the color pills. That can't be right, maybe it was a tablespoon, and one cup of room temperature water. Naw!! It was a half cup. (?) I had better read the instructions, I reckon. Yup, those are now out in the trash bin with the egg-drying-box holes punched through the instructions. Now, a half roll of type one 3-M scotch tape later, I had a drying box with half the instructions on it. I need to dig out those little hole punches I had pitched with part of the instructions that are not in Spanish. Okay, NOW we were ready to dye eggs. Pretty sure. Some of those color pills don't dissolve all the way, is that normal?

So I have all the eggs dyed with little stickers on some and I drew faces on some others. The eggs aren't even out of the kitchen yet, and I have already lost three. Tomorrow won't be good for me to find these. I better have the neighbor kids come find them. Should I dye one that isn't cooked? You know, just for fun?

We are Learnin' Stuff!!

***

Well, I just knew it was going to be one of those days when I got up this morning. Right off the bat I got dressed and at first things went well, then stuff started to happen. I put on my Fitbit to count my steps because I need every step I can get. I went into the kitchen to get my coffee and tripped over a cat that we don't own. I racked up 63 steps tryin' to catch myself and get somebody else's cat out of the kitchen. Seems that cat gets excited, has no idea where he is or how to get back from there.

Almost 100 steps by the time I got to my coffee, had to rest for 30 minutes.

Decided to do a few things on the boat and accidentally bumped the trailer a little bit. The trailer tongue wheel rolled off the cinder block and hit the ground. Racked up about 50 more steps just getting away from that. All I wanted was the gas cap. Gosh, now I have to rest again.

While I was restin', thought I'd get a deposit ready for the bank and write out checks for some bills. Had to write two checks twice before I got the bills right. Sometimes you know you should have stayed in bed, but it's too late now. I headed to the post office to drop off the bills, stepped out of the car, went to step back to shut the door and was standing on my shoestring. That didn't work out well, racked up another 75 steps and didn't even turn loose of the car door. It turned out to be a bigger deal than just a waltz with the door, it was more like the boogie-woogie. Heck, I had to get back in the car to rest. I decided to drop the mail in the drop box, so I didn't have to get out of the car. I am starting to worry about getting to the bank for the deposit. Got to the bank in time, and as I started headed for the house, I got an ass chewin' from my car because I didn't step on the brake as soon as it thought I should. Probably a good thing I didn't ride my scooter or go for a walk on the treadmill today.

Good times, I reckon.

***

Made some jello the other day and added a can of fruit cocktail to make it gooder. I also put some of those little marshmallows in my half because Georgie doesn't like marshmallows. I don't know if there is a special time to add those little marshmallows, but my jello sure didn't look like the ones the ladies bring to the family reunions. I dropped them straight in so I wouldn't forget. I guess the heat has somethin' to do with the way they react. They kinda turned red, same as the jello. Ya know, after a few days in the fridge that stuff turns into elastic. I dug a spoonful out. Ya' know how ya' pull your pizza way up in the air until that string of cheese turns loose and then ya' swirl it around to wrap it up so it doesn't get stuck on your chin when ya' take the first bite? Well, that doesn't work with jello and marshmallows. I pulled that jello up about 10 inches and it snapped like a bungee cord left out all winter, and my spoonful of jello smacked up against our Keurig coffee maker where it stuck. Of course, as I tried to peel it off, it decided to land on the counter and hang out. I finally got that sucker in the bowl I had planned for it to go in, and felt like I needed to put a lid on it to keep it in there. I had second thoughts about getting another spoonful. I cleaned off the counter and the Keurig and realized why Georgie doesn't care much for marshmallows.

Yup!! Learnin' Stuff.

***

Tried somethin' different for breakfast this mornin'. I sliced up some mushrooms, a slice of bologna cut into small pieces and fried 'em in butter. This is goin' to be good stuff. I had the burner up a little high and I was hurryin' to get my eggs in there. Well, we buy our eggs in a clear plastic 18-pack at

Costco. Couldn't get that egg carton to open! Reached over and stirred the goodies I had going and decided I was tryin' to open the wrong side of the egg carton. Now it's getting smoky, so I'm speedin' up my efforts to get those eggs out. Oops! I forgot how slimy eggs are to get off the floor. I can't take time to address a cleanup crew at this time, not until I get my eggs in that pan! There! Now, about that egg I launched onto the kitchen floor. It was strung all over the kitchen and I dragged my oxygen hose through it a few times. By the time I got it cleaned up, my eggs and coffee were cold.

Thinkin' about it later, I reckon I should have taken the pan off the burner and taken my time gettin' the eggs out.

Rice Krispies tomorrow.

I'm Learnin Stuff!

***

Not quite sure why, but sometimes in the fall I have a tendency to test my reflexes. I used to be pretty quick and able to get away from a rake I stepped on. That is no longer true. I have been testing myself over the years and have reported on it here on Facebook a few times.

Usually when I take a step and don't notice the rake laying there, it just whops me good and rings a few bells. I get my eyesight back for a short spell, but only see stars.

Now instead of feeling like I just got hit with a rake handle, I feel like I fell down the stairs carryin' a washer and dryer. It takes me a little bit to catch my breath because I am not used to movin' so fast (it was only a step or two).

Yup!!! Will never fully learn. :)

Teenage boy steps out on his grandparent's porch and sees grandpa sittin' in his rocker and says, "Grandpa, what are you doing sitting out on the porch without your pants on?" Grandpa says, "Well last week I sat out here with no shirt on and I got a stiff neck. This was grandma's idea."

Made it back from Georgia's family reunion so you all are going to have to put up with me for a bit longer.

We had a great trip and I found out a few things. One thing is that the elevation in Wyoming is not my friend. 7,000 feet has me maxed out. From Idaho to the other side of Wyoming the elevation goes up about 6,500 feet and just before it drops into Colorado, it is a little over 8,000. I found out that at anything over 6,500 feet, I get Alzheimer's. I do alright until the car door opens and lets in that thin air. We always stop at Little America and get an ice cream cone. Heck, everyone does, pretty sure. Stopped on the way back home with our grandkids. Everyone was gettin' on shoes and pickin' up stuff they kicked out of the car. Georgie gathered up Matthew while Audrey and I waited for them on the sidewalk by the door. All the doors on the car were shut and Georgie pushed her lock the car button, and it wouldn't work. "Here, let me try it with my lock the car button, yours must be broken." Ahaaa!! My keys were in the ignition. I left the stinkin' car runnin and was gonna go get myself an ice cream. What? Was it that thin air? Gosh, I hope I wasn't an idiot all the time we were gone. I thought I just did that at our house.

Yup!!! Good Times.

***

I have learned over the last week that there are some things that are just plain hard to do. Like putting your wallet into or taking it out of your hip pocket while driving and not unbuckling your seatbelt. Holy smoke, that is like trying to stuff a wet noodle down the back of your spandex bicycle shorts on the move. Mom always told me nothing is impossible, but they didn't have spandex then.

***

My wife bought one of those chef salads the other day at the grocery store, ya' know the ones that are in a little container with a clear lid, and it comes with dressing and a fork. She brought it home and we had it for supper, it was really pretty good. She liked the plastic container and thought it would be nice to take lunches to work in. I cleaned it up for her Saturday while she was out 'yard-saling' with the neighbors. Did you know those things are not dishwasher safe? I was pretty sure that thing was square when I put it in there. When I took it out, the top looked like a folded over diamond T pickup truck and flat as a piece of paper. The bottom didn't fare so well either. I have seen a piece of wadded up tin foil that had better days. I chucked it in the garbage and so far, it hasn't been missed. One of these days I will figure out what can and can't be washed in the washer.

One day I was cleaning a bunch of stuff that was on shelves... little knick-knack stuff. Those little white doves that feel kinda sandy. Thems doesn't do well in the dishwasher either. They disappear completely. I did a lot of talkin' to convince myself that I put them in there and then I did a lot of talkin' tryin' to explain the white film all over the dishes to Georgie. Cleaned them right down the drain.

Yup!!! I'M JUST LEARNIN' STUFF!

***

Nothing like making an old fella feel good for a while. I had to go into the Honda dealer to get registration stickers for our 4-wheelers. There was a young, good lookin', long haired, blue eyed chic in there doin' some shoppin'. When I first walked in, she looked at me and smiled from across the room and I smiled back. I was standing at the counter and a few minutes later, she came walking by slowly and smiled again so I smiled back. She was a fox. She went over to look at some clothes, picked something out, came back, standing behind me in line. I turned and smiled at her as I was headed out. She smiled back again. All this time she is lookin' me right in the eye. I got to the car, started it, looked in the rear-view mirror to back out. I raised my head enough to check my face. Did I have a chunk of lettuce stuck to my teeth that she was lookin at? Nope, no lettuce. I backed out slowly feelin' good. The sun kinda shone in the car as I glanced in the mirror, and there it was, glistening in the afternoon sun, a big, long, silver hair growing straight out the edge of my right ear. That thing was so long I thought it was tucked under the neckline of my t-shirt.

I had been thinking that this young gal kept getting closer to see if maybe this old fella was kinda cute and I was feelin' pretty good about myself. Nope, just that big, long, silver hair jammed down my t-shirt attached to my ear. I betcha she was tryin' to see if it was a new hearing aid device I could carry in my pocket.

Good Times Still.

***

You think life will go back to the same ol' thing when all your company leaves. But...

The very next day after my sister-in-law and her hubby left, my life went right back to the old ways. I had a pot of coffee brewing in one of those Bunn coffee makers and decided to fill the sugar bowl. I snatched the container off the counter and turned to open the cupboard behind me. The sugar container hit the coffee ground holder on the coffee maker, knocked it onto the counter and the water was still coming out of the maker. The grounds holder was about a third full of water so there was hot water and coffee grounds all over the kitchen. With a few choice words I got that cleaned up.

That evening, I went to get a cup of coffee, grabbed the pot and realized Georgie had one brewing that wasn't finished yet. So... more coffee on the counter. Decided not to throw out any choice words this time because Georgie doesn't like that, and I was within striking distance. I got it cleaned up as well. Sure went through a lot of coffee that day.

The next day, we were eating in the living room and one of those little fruit flies was hangin' out around my milk, so I shooed it away with my hand and knocked over my milk. Yup, a few more choice words and a talkin' to about my potty mouth. It was really hard to try to convince Georgie that those bad words just flew out so fast I couldn't control them.

So, now I have cleaned the whole area around the coffee maker and the floor mopped, twice, you know. I then cleaned the stand in the living room thoroughly to make up for my insane choice of words. The rest of this week has been pretty good. My potty mouth has been under control and things have gone well. I really have to work on that mouth some.

***

Holy Smoke, I have been working on our basement apartment, getting it ready to rent and trying to fill a hole in the wall with some putty. Talk about a job! I would stuff in the putty and it would push back out, so I would push it in again.

Yup, back out it came! I jammed that stuff back in and out it came. Damn stuff, I stuck a pencil in, wiggled it around and jammed it in again. Must be an air pocket in it. I wet my jammer down so it would slide off the putty, jammed some putty more in the hole and threw a piece of tape over it so it wouldn't come out. Took the tape off after a while and let it dry out. Pretty cool, looks brand new, except for that little piece right....... Chit!

This is like trying to put Chapstick on a cat. Sanded it down and only have half the hole now. Wonder if I can fill that with paint? Naw, better not. Another ten minutes and a few choice words and we got-r-done.

I still have to work on choosing better words!

***

Did ya' ever have that dream where you finally find that treasure hidden deep in the cushions of the back seat of an old couch that has been in an old house for years and years? Maybe under the seats of a 1949 Chrysler. When I was little, I always thought that would be so cool. Maybe I was expecting too much, I sure thought my ship would come in and I would find great things in those old couches or under old car seats.

Well, I finally got my chance. Someone left one of those 27-foot reclinin' couches downstairs in our apartment. We had a new screen door in the back, so now it wouldn't make it out without taking it apart. It wasn't any good, so I started taking it apart, trying to hurry so I could get it all done before Georgie got home (so I could claim the treasure all to myself). I was into that couch so deep nothin' but my fat little feet were hangin out. Had myself one of those little Maglite flashlights so I could see everything.

Well, my ship was a submarine with a screen door. I found a good pair of fingernail clippers, a sticky dime, a handful of

Sweet Tarts, a few pieces of popcorn jammed on the sides of the cushions, a couple bag ties and half a dozen crayons. So, I guess I will share my treasure with Georgie after all (I would have done that anyway. :))

Oh yeah, I found that jigsaw puzzle piece that was always missin'!! Maybe, just maybe, my treasure is a 1949 Chrysler. This is America ya' know. My Dream.

***

I guess some of the old habits I had years ago have no room in today's world.

I would get out of the car and as I was about to enter into a store or the house, I would feel on the outside of my britches pocket to make sure I put the car keys in there. The keys for our car now is like shovin' a brick in your pocket with a switchblade duct-taped to the side of it.

While putting the keys in my pocket once I accidentally hit the button that opened the back of the car at Fred Meyer and dang near knocked over an old lady that was headed to her car with a couple bags of groceries. She sure was surprised! (So was I!) And I was glad I wasn't very close to her, I might have been eatin' dirt. Then one other time I felt to see if the keys were there and hit that little button that opens the switchblade. Holy Smoke! It is a good thing that it's only a key that flies out, I could have been in deep trouble. I still had a heck of a time tryin' to get that out of my pocket, kinda like yankin' a pigeon through a piggy bank slot! I got it though. I did that once more and set off the alarm system. I had no idea that was even on the brick. I couldn't figure out why the car came unglued all by itself. Good thing Georgie was right there.

If I do that again and the car starts up, I'm drivin' the truck. It's old, made of steel and has a good old-fashioned key. Yup, by golly!!

***

I'm not a very smart man, as Forest would say, but I don't think all this smart stuff they have nowadays is a smart idea. Take my wife's phone, for instance. It is a "smart" phone. you can ask it a question and it will give you the answer. Hmm. Do kids get to take these to class?

You can also ask for directions and it will tell you where to go. Yup! I didn't need a smartphone to tell me where to go. I have had plenty of ordinary people tell me that, and it didn't cost $700.00 bucks and then a monthly 'friendship fee.'

Then, we have a "smart" TV. How about that! You can leave it on one station before you go to bed and the next morning it will be on a station that you watched two or three times the previous week. So much for privacy, huh!! This thing will also adjust the volume automatically. If you couldn't hear yesterday, it thinks you're deaf again today. This fancy smart TV also has a 'friendship fee' of approximately 80 bucks a month.

We also have a "smart" car. Now here ya' go!!! This thing not only gets you from point A to point B but gives you all the conveniences you just left at home. Have you ever wondered why the dash in your new car is so big? Yup! There is a woman under there that talks to ya'! Tells ya what ya did wrong... an old-fashioned backseat driver... but under the dash so you can't see her. Our car tells everything, I mean everything... you crossed over the white line, there's another car beside you. It yells at you if you have the car in reverse and someone or his cat walks behind you and even has a security camera so no one can put the sneak on ya from behind. You can also answer your phone through the radio. How about that!!!

Although these cars have everything you need and all the safety things, they are more dangerous than the old ones.

221

People who drive them seem to depend on the gadgets in the car to wake them up every now and then. These cars are made of plastic and catch on fire once in a while. It is a good thing, I think, if you just let it burn. By the time the fire burns out and cools off, you can pick up what is left and put it in your pocket. Saved yourself a towing charge. These cars also cost around $30,000 bucks, just a tad less than our house did. These also come with a monthly 'friendship fee' of approximately $120.00 a month.

So there ya have it, all this "smart" stuff. Smart phone, smart TV, and smart car. All my mama had was us four kids, a "smart aleck," a "smarty pants", a "smart ass" and a "dumb ass". Yikes!!!

***

Went into the kitchen to turn some things off earlier today while I had my oxygen hose on. I turned off the coffee pot and headed back to the livingroom but my oxygen hose got wrapped around somethin' so I gave it a couple quick jerks, you know, because sometimes it will just come undone, and it saves me a trip back into the kitchen. I saw one of the cats headed out of there pretty quick and my hose was still stuck under somethin'. So I pulled harder and it gave way... sure was a lot of racket goin' on in the kitchen! I better go check. Hmmm... Evidently my hose went around the broom handle AND the mop, slingshot the broom (and mop) across the floor, kinda swept the kitchen floor and then mopped it at the same time with the cat's water.

I think my wife might be proud of me this time, pretty sure! If you don't hear from me for a while, you might have to check the homeless center or somethin'.

Boy, I swear, for someone that doesn't have much oxygen in their system, sometimes when I sneeze it is a force to be reckoned with. This time I was lucky... just blasted my pill bottle across the computer desk. I reckon it is the amount of particles you have left over in your mouth from just finishing dinner that blasts the stuff off the walls or all the grandkid's pictures off the fridge... kinda like a grandpa 12 gauge. I am afraid to turn around in case someone is standing there and I blow their britches off or somethin'. I just look to the sky before sneezing and thank the Lord I have enough air to continue to sneeze and hope my teeth stay in. So far, I have been blessed. Those teeth have stuck with me through many ordeals.

I can't imagine what it would be like sittin' in Texas Roadhouse if my teeth made an exit from my mouth and scooted across the table at 800 feet per second, coming to rest in front of some lady sittin' at another table.

Reckon I can feel good about having to just wash the walls or the fridge instead of getting quarantined for 10 days while some lady goes through rabies shots. Yikes!!!

***

I do not like this computer age.

We have one of those home burglar alarm system do-dads. You know what I'm talkin' about... if somethin' happens the alarm fellas call the police, fire department, or ambulance instead of gettin' ya' a burger and callin' your wife.

Well, ours was makin' this terrible noise about once every 30 seconds and said it had low batteries. Hey, I could fix that. I went to the door, tore that sucker apart and put in some new batteries. Nope, that wasn't it. It still made that God-awful noise every 30 seconds to tell me somethin' was wrong. Aha! It must be the part on the wall, so I tore the cover off that sucker and believe me, there was no battery in there needing replaced. AND I couldn't get that dang cover back together!

I was losin' patience, so I took the whole thing off the wall, unplugged it and proceeded to complete my fixin' stuff. I must have pushed somethin' with my knee because alarms started goin' off, flashin' red and the phone starts ringin'. I grabbed the phone and it was the guy at the burger joint. I was thinkin' about runnin' out the back when the doorbell rings. I glance out the winda and Holy Chit! It's the Police. I was on the phone with the guy from the burger place as I answered the door. These were the nicest police and understood the spot I was in. One of them asked for an ID so she would know if I belonged here or not. I went to get my wallet to give her my driver's license and she said, "Yup, it says that this is you and you live here." I told her that was good, at least I was sleepin' at the right house!

They laughed as they headed for their cars and she said they liked these kinds of calls. :) I thanked them and apologized. I calmed down somewhat and with help from the fella on the phone, I was able to get it going again. He also told me the 'low battery' was a glitch in their system and it really wasn't low.

I ran to fish the batteries out of the garbage. I'm good to go now. I really do love life. Honest.

Good times!!!!!!!!!!!

ABOUT THE AUTHOR

Stan Callantine was born in Bozeman, Montana in January 1950. He was the third of four children and grew up exploring the forests and rivers of Montana, developing a love of animals and the out-of-doors that persisted his whole life.

No matter his age, he continued to approach life as a young & curious boy who was always looking for adventures, and then telling the stories to everyone who would listen, maybe adding in a line or two to really get them rolling.

He lived his adult life in Idaho but found himself always calling Montana "home" and telling these stories to keep his memories of Montana alive. Though he missed living in Montana, Stan soon fell in love with the mountains, plains and high deserts of Idaho where he hunted elk, deer, coyotes and waterfowl.

He raised his two children, Jason and Nicole with the love of his life, Georgie in Pocatello, Idaho in their home of 40 years. Stan lived the rest of his life in Pocatello and continued to make beloved goofy memories until his body was simply unable to carry on another day in April of 2021. He left behind his son, daughter, six grandchildren and one great-grandson. He is dearly missed by so many.

"Laughter is one of the best medicines available to everyone. My wish is that something in this book will bring a smile to your face. If you see someone without a smile, give them yours."

~ Stan Callantine
1950-2021